IN THE PARISH
OF THE POOR

*Father Jean-Bertrand Aristide during Mass
in St. Jean Bosco Church, 1987.*

IN THE PARISH
OF THE POOR

Writings from Haiti

Jean-Bertrand Aristide

Translated and edited by Amy Wilentz

ORBIS BOOKS

Maryknoll, New York 10545

Second Printing, March 1991

The Catholic Foreign Mission Society of America (Maryknoll) recruits and trains people for overseas missionary service. Through Orbis Books, Maryknoll aims to foster the international dialogue that is essential to mission. The books published, however, reflect the opinions of their authors and are not meant to represent the official position of the society.

Library of Congress Cataloging-in-Publication Data

Aristide, Jean-Bertrand.
    [Selections. English. 1990]
    In the parish of the poor: writings from Haiti / Jean-Bertrand
Aristide; translated and edited by Amy Wilentz.
      p. cm.
    Contents: A letter to my brothers andsisters—A call to
holiness—Walking in the light of Christ—"We have come from far
away"—Let the flood descend.
    ISBN 0-88344-682-0
    1. Aristide, Jean-Bertrand. 2. Poor—Haiti. 3. Persecution—
Haiti. 4. Catholic Church—Sermons. 5. Sermons, English—
Translations from French. 6. Sermons, French—Translations into
English. I. Wilentz, Amy. II. Title.
BX4705.A7235   1990
282'.7294—dc20
                                       90-42004
                                         CIP

To the martyrs of St. Jean Bosco.
You will forever live in my memory.

CONTENTS

Aristide with street boys.

FOREWORD

Events in Haiti often proceed in such a rush, with such highs and lows, that it is sometimes difficult to perceive their general direction. At the end of a dizzying and dangerous road to democracy, an election-day massacre suddenly looms like a terrifying roadblock. In the midst of dictatorship and repression, a frail sprout of democracy somehow pushes forward. A man may think that he has attained the zenith of his career in Haiti, only to find himself the next day plunged into an abyss of shame and degradation. Another may find himself lost, abandoned, discarded, marginalized, and expelled, only to discover that this very state represents the peak of his ambitions.

The latter has been the case of Father Jean-Bertrand Aristide. Just before and for four years after the 1986 fall of the Haitian dictator Jean-Claude Duvalier, Father Aristide, now 37, became a bellwether for the popular democratic movement in Haiti. The most outspoken member of Ti Legliz (literally, the little church, the progressive wing of the Roman Catholic Church in Haiti), the charismatic and high-strung priest was the most public of Haiti's liberation clergy. Pè Titid, as he is known affectionately, suffered when the Haitian people suffered, and rose to great heights when they did.

Every time a government with popular support seemed to be edging near to power, Aristide was there to hearten and inspire the Haitian people. When the people were beaten and killed by the armed forces during a series of brutal regimes, he spoke out against the abuses at great personal peril; when the people were manning barricades across the country to protect its fledgling pro-democracy movement, he encouraged them.

Every time he said Mass, his church—St. Jean Bosco, on the

edge of the La Saline slum in Port-au-Prince, Haiti's capital—
was filled to capacity with people involved in the movement. He
gave hope to his parishioners from the slums, and his words
helped them to understand in an analytic as well as a symbolic
way the structure of the system that had entrapped them. In a
country so degraded by its recent history that in its political
ranks hypocrites preponderate, Aristide remained one of the
very few public figures in whom the Haitian people had confidence. At a time when few had the courage to speak out on the
people's behalf, and no one else had the forum in which to take
that great risk, Father Aristide was never reluctant to come
forward.

Haiti is a very Catholic country (although almost all the peasantry and many of the city dwellers also worship in Vodun, or
voodoo); only recently have Protestant sects made themselves
felt to any great degree throughout the countryside. The
Church's presence can be felt at almost every stage of a Haitian's
life. As in other Latin American countries, the Church is the
educator of first resort; all young men and women who come
into the capital from the provinces with any degree of learning
have been taught by sisters or fathers. Most of the best schools
in the country are run by the Catholic Church. For poor peasants, a life in the Church is often the only alternative to a pun-
ishing life on the farm—I know more than one Haitian priest of
great erudition whose parents were both illiterate peasants.
Aristide's parents were both from the peasant class.

For centuries, the Haitian bishop was the focus of provincial
life and a figure of deep respect. Similarly, the curate (along
with the Vodun priest) was at the core of Haitian villages and
neighborhoods. The curate helped the very poor, developing
community projects, building housing, running food programs,
offering charity. He was a source—often the only source—of
monies for the people. The old saying in Creole is *"Aprè Bon
Dye, se pè-a"* ("After God, the priest"). He was also a teacher,
along with the other parish priests and nuns.

But with the growth in the 1970s of the base ecclesial communities—or *ti kominite legliz* (TKL) in Creole—the Church all
over Haiti began to change radically, and so did people's per-

ception of the Church. Now, with the upsurge in grassroots work being done by the TKLs, the curate grew less influential. The concept of self-help—which already figured largely in the Haitian-African workgroup, or *konbit*—was encouraged by the TKLs, and committed lay people became in the peasants' eyes almost as important as the priest.

In Port-au-Prince in particular, the TKLs have been crucial to the continuing legitimacy and popular strength of the Catholic Church. (A little under a fifth of Haiti's population resides in Port-au-Prince.) The TKLs came of age in the late 1970s, just at the time when Protestant sects like the Latter Day Saints and the Pentecostals were pouring money into Haiti and luring thousands of Haitians away from Catholicism with their wealth, their smaller congregations, and their easier access to the minister.

Though mothers and grandmothers and uncles with gray hair and great-grandfathers would never have dreamed of leaving the Catholic Church and the priest whom they had known since he was a little altar boy, young people in droves were moving into Protestantism or abandoning religion altogether. The young failed to see how the Church, which too often taught only acceptance, submission, and prayer, could help them emerge from their desperate straits. They did not see prayer as a useful tool in a life that promised no education, no job, ill health, scant housing, little food, and the same thing again for their children.

The TKLs brought the young and the desperate back into the Church in Haiti because the community groups gave these people a new understanding of the possibility for change. In the city, Father Aristide helped initiate a number of TKLs, for young people, for students, for young women. St. Jean Bosco became a gathering place for the youth groups, and the small church, for years sparsely attended by older women and little children, was suddenly full of young people. Every Tuesday evening, there was a youth Mass, in which these lay people took over, and Aristide ministered only nominally.

At that time, there was an enormous feeling of hope around St. Jean Bosco. The young people from the various TKLs met there, and the progressive clergy were in and out all day long.

Change was being organized, palpably, or so it seemed at the time. The young people were always engaged in heated political debate; they were always drawing up plans for one project or another; they were developing literacy programs; there was a sense of excitement and potential in their lives.

Aristide worked with them, but he drew his spiritual strength from—and breathed it into—a wider congregation. His Sunday sermons, full of Creole wordplay and biblical invective against the dictatorship, were famous in Port-au-Prince in the months and weeks before Jean-Claude Duvalier fell. As the regime was crumbling, popular unrest heated up around the country but was slow in coming to Port-au-Prince; from his pulpit, Aristide helped encourage the young people of the capital to join in the demonstrations that eventually led to Duvalier's downfall. In all this, the Church hierarchy acquiesced. In those days, they saw Aristide as a spirit infuser, a useful consciousness-raiser.

Then Duvalier left, and the hierarchy's attitude began to change.

In late 1985 and early 1986, the Church—from top to bottom—had played a major role in the Haitian and foreign establishments' final rejection of President-for-Life Jean-Claude Duvalier—the son and successor of Dr. François Duvalier, who had come to power more than 29 years before and who died in 1971. In 1983, Pope John Paul II had visited Haiti. Although to the astonishment of many in Ti Legliz, the pope agreed to meet the young Duvalier, John Paul was nonetheless shocked by the disparity between the rich and poor in the poorest nation in the Western Hemisphere; before leaving, he pronounced the (to Haitians) famous words: "Things must change."

The Haitian Episcopal Conference took his lead and spoke out gently against Duvalier, and then more and more urgently as popular protest gathered. Duvalier, after all, was now seen as anachronistic in a world that seemed already to be turning toward democracy. Ronald Reagan's spin-makers were calling it "People Power." The United States State Department—on a roll with its decision to abandon former American friend Ferdinand Marcos in the Philippines—was anxious to part with its other pet island dictator quickly and with as little structural change as possible. The Haitian Army had little use for Jean-Claude Duvalier, and even the Tontons Macoute, the vicious paramilitary group set up by his father, were not particularly concerned with the son's fate now that they were firmly entrenched on the Haitian scene.

In other words, the Church joined in with the rest of the establishment in Haiti. With some of its inspiration taken from Aristide's preachings, the vast outpouring of popular protest finally overtook Port-au-Prince, and the full spectrum of Haitian society managed to oust the dictator.

But, as Father Aristide said later about another deposed head of state: "The driver is gone, but the car is still here, loaded down with the weapons of Duvalierism." Indeed, the structure of the society remained unchanged. The Tontons Macoute, for example, were still abroad, and a brief and violent attempt on the part of the people to bring these men to a swift, street justice was understandably quashed by some well-chosen words from the Haitian bishops.

Yet the bishops offered no alternative to the street tribunals and put no serious pressure on the new government to prosecute criminals from the old regime. They abandoned Aristide and his colleagues, who were intent on publicly continuing the fight against Duvalierism. Perhaps some of the bishops felt themselves uncomfortably implicated in the whole messy affair of the *ancien regime*, and hence wished to let sleeping dogs lie.

In spite of the trust he inspires in the Haitian people—or perhaps because of it—Aristide has been seen during the past few turbulent years of Haitian history as a dangerous character by outside observers: foreign diplomats, Western reporters, the Vatican. When, during the summer of 1987, it became clear that Aristide (along with other Ti Legliz priests and popular leaders) was involved in helping to organize demonstrations and protests against an increasingly repressive regime, those outside observers became more and more wary of him. They saw in him a kind of demagogic popular leader who could carry off a socialist revolution: "radical firebrand" was the epithet used for Father Aristide in U.S. embassy cables.

The wariness eventually translated into a kind of loose cam-

MEV PULEO

paign against him; it is clear from U.S. embassy cables at the time, cables that were sent along to the Vatican, that the American government would have preferred the priest's absence from the scene. Similarly, the papal nuncio in Haiti—who had served there since before the fall of the Duvalier dynasty—was rarely reluctant, at least in private, to express his displeasure with Aristide.

In what now seems an astonishingly short time, Aristide's order, the Salesians, took several actions against him. Beginning in 1986, they attempted to silence him, to move him out of his parish; they threatened him with expulsion and exile, and finally, in December of 1988, with Vatican approval, they expelled him from the order for mixing politics and pulpit. He was charged, more exactly, with preaching violence and "class struggle." (Cardinal Miguel Obando y Bravo of Nicaragua, a Salesian who openly used his pulpit to oppose the Sandinista government of Daniel Ortega, has never been chastised by the order.)

While the Church hierarchy was pursuing its own canonical offensive against Aristide and Ti Legliz, the government of Gen. Henri Namphy and his supporters among Duvalier's former cronies were also on the attack. It seemed spectacular when Aristide, along with three other progressive clergymen, was ambushed at a roadblock and narrowly escaped assassination in 1987. Yet that assault paled in comparison with the all-out blitzkreig against St. Jean Bosco a year later, in which parishioners were killed and the church burned down, and from which, once again, several progressive lay people as well as Father Aristide barely escaped alive.

It is important to understand some Haitian church history if one wishes to fathom the reasons for the Haitian bishops' intransigent behavior toward Aristide over the past few years. The indigenous Haitian episcopacy was created by Dr. Duvalier ("Papa Doc") in 1966, after a protracted and bitter feud with the Holy See, which the dictator documented in his overlong and shamelessly self-congratulatory book, *Memoirs of a Third-World Leader* (Paris: Librarie Hachette, 1969). Papa Doc correctly perceived that the strongest opposition he faced—outside the Haitian Army, which he had already decimated and infiltrated—was from the foreign-led Catholic Church.

He expelled the Jesuits and the Holy Ghost Fathers, and summarily exiled the bishop of Gonaïves, but remained dissatisfied. As in all other areas, Dr. Duvalier wanted complete control. In 1966, the Vatican, exhausted by Duvalier's dogged combativeness and already moving more generally toward an indigenous clergy—allowed Duvalier to choose four Haitian bishops, who were duly consecrated. A photograph on page 286 of the lavishly illustrated *Memoirs* shows Duvalier surrounded by the new archbishop of Port-au-Prince and the three other new Haitian bishops.

I recognize two of the four Haitians: Emmanuel Constant, bishop of Gonaïves, and François Wolf Ligondé, archbishop of Port-au-Prince. They retain today the positions they held under Papa Doc. Neither ever used his protected position of authority to denounce or even to discourage the brutal, deathly repression that Papa Doc directed. Instead, they included the dictator in their public prayers. Almost all the other members of the Haitian Episcopal Conference, as it exists today, were named by Duvalier or his son, Jean-Claude.

In Haiti, in other words, there are no progressive bishops. (In 1987, in the heat of a politically charged summer, one did raise a lonely voice, but he was quickly brought into line.) In Haiti, there are no bishops who espouse any serious form of liberation theology. In Haiti, there are no bishops who come to the defense of Ti Legliz when it is threatened by secular powers. This lack of progressives at the highest level of the hierarchy has made Haiti an exceptional case in Latin America in the past two decades and has polarized the Haitian Church—though the Haitian conference may not remain exceptional for long, as progressive bishops throughout the hemisphere retire and are replaced by conservatives.

As Haiti wandered down the perilous path toward elections in 1987, violence erupted from the Tontons Macoute and from the Army, both of which felt threatened by the prospect of popular empowerment. The Church said nothing. Father Aristide

and the three other clergymen were attacked on a lonely highway and almost killed by these same two forces, and the bishops'
conference remained silent. I ran into Bishop Constant at the
hospital where the four wounded priests were being treated (in
a rare gesture of ecclesial solidarity, Constant and the Papal
Nuncio had accompanied them in the ambulance on their trip
back to the capital), but he had nothing to say. Six days after
the ambush, the bishops released a message critical of Ti Legliz.
The criticism was based on the hierarchy's favorite straw man,
namely, that Ti Legliz was attempting to establish a parallel and
separate "People's Church" in Haiti. Many in Ti Legliz believed
that the bishops were cutting them loose, in effect saying that
Ti Legliz was no longer under the protection of the bishops.

While electoral offices were shot up and homes of electoral
officials burned, the bishops held their tongues. Only after the
horrifying massacre on election day did they finally speak out.
A year later, after Aristide's church was burned and his parishioners speared and macheted to death, the bishops' conference
waited a full two weeks before condemning the attack. Not one
of them sided with Father Aristide in his ensuing battle with the
Salesians. In fact, a Salesian spokesman in the United States
said that the Haitian bishops had advised the Salesians to issue
the order of expulsion.

Aristide was not the only progressive priest to suffer during
this period. Other young and popular liberation theologians
were silenced and moved out of their parishes for minor offenses
tolerated among more conservative clergy. Older progressive
priests also were reprimanded or, at best, given the Church's
cold shoulder. Antoine Adrien and William Smarth, two well-
known priests who had been exiled during Papa Doc's 1969
expulsion of the Holy Ghost Fathers, and who had then tirelessly
worked against Duvalierism from their small office in Brooklyn,
were given no parish upon their return to Haiti in 1986 and were
never supported in their work. They were wounded along with
Aristide in the highway ambush. I remember seeing the gray-
haired Father Adrien with his head swollen from the stoning
and his bloodied eye bandaged.

By 1990, still without a parish, living in a residence at the edges of the teeming, bustling St. Martin slum, Father Adrien had become—through various odd twists and turns of politics, fate, and character—the nominal head of the hastily patched-together Unity Assembly, a team of twelve prominent political and social leaders trying to oust the increasingly bloody Duvalierist dictator, Gen. Prosper Avril. Adrien was the moving force and negotiator behind the eventually successful effort, and he also helped coordinate and organize the civilian government that succeeded the general.

The turning point in that campaign was the symbolic funeral Mass said by Adrien for Roseline Vaval, an 11-year-old girl who had just been killed by the Army. In what appeared to be a Church-wide directive, no church in Port-au-Prince would agree to open its doors for Father Adrien's service, yet thousands came, at the risk of their lives, to hear him say the Mass. During a period of cruel street violence and unrest, Father Adrien was forced to say the Mass outdoors in the Bel-Air slum—or not to say it at all. He chose to say the Mass. That Mass turned into the bloody but triumphant march that effectively ended the military regime.

Father Aristide, meanwhile, was still on the scene, a feat of amazing political survival. He had been ousted from his order, banned from saying public Mass, cut off from Church funding. A year after it had been sent to Rome, his canonical appeal was still pending. One might have thought that, abandoned, discarded, marginalized, silenced, and kicked out, he would have lost the sway he once had had over the Haitian people. The Church had publicly reviled him, as had the rest of the Haitian establishment. By all rights, he should have been at the nadir of his powers. But just as no one can prop up for very long the strongman who has no popular base, neither can anyone take away the power of those whose legitimacy is based on true popular support. (Only their own mistakes can rob them of their force.)

Thus, at that crucial juncture in 1990, it was in part Father Aristide's dramatic and public support that helped make Father Adrien's long-term consensus-building work successful. Over the radio waves, Aristide kept the momentum of Adrien's funeral

MEV PULEO

march going. Aristide's energetic and eloquent radio broadcasts kept the Haitian people out on the streets and mobilized at their barricades at a time of great political tension. Their willingness to risk their lives for a change in government gave credence to the Unity Assembly's claims of popular support. In part because of Adrien and Aristide, two priests largely rejected by the hierarchical Church, Gen. Avril was forced to leave and to hand power over to a civilian government. Ironically, Father Adrien's honorable and intelligent guidance of the campaign to oust the military regime was subsequently used as a bit of polish with which to shine up the tarnished image of the Church in Haiti.

Throughout this period, I was in Haiti on and off, writing a book. It turned out that Father Aristide would have an important place in that book, but when I first started my research, I did not know that. The book in a way took shape around him: He was finding his way toward the person whom he truly would become, and as I observed him, I realized that around him had crystallized many of the controversies and trends that would face Haiti in the years to come.

For me, Father Aristide began as a mystery. His charismatic style was unfamiliar, his Creole, sharp, biting, initially hard to decipher. His appeal seemed inexplicable. He is a small, frail-looking person, far from a commanding presence at first sight, yet young people and matrons and doctors and lawyers and the very poor all waited patiently to see him, around the clock, it seemed, every day. His reactions to brutality and repression and dictatorship were emotional and visceral at the outset, and only later analytic. I couldn't figure him out.

He has been criticized by his fellow clergy, including members of Ti Legliz, for his rashness and his impulsive behavior. He is not a natural strategist. He is not much of a team player, though he has learned to play ball at crucial moments. He believes in inspiration and trusts that inspiration will lead him down the right path for the long term. He believes that his own inspiration flows from an instinctive analysis of the facts of the situation in Haiti. He believes that, in the end, those colleagues who criticize him will come to see the ultimate wisdom of his seemingly hasty actions or words. He takes more care than is often believed to act responsibly toward those whom he still considers his congregation: the Haitian people. For the most part, his political judgments and predictions, often vehemently expressed, have turned out to be correct. Yet, as he once said, "Who wants to be proved right by the blood of the people?"

His detractors in Ti Legliz have finally come to understand Aristide's role in the movement toward democracy and national liberation as a limited one, but crucial. He in many senses stands for the people, inasmuch as any one man can ever do. His reaction to a plan, or a strategy, or an announcement, is likely to be the people's general reaction. He always seems to know, for example, whether or not a strike will succeed and this is not just because he is well informed. Ti Legliz and the popular movement can often test their strategems by running them past Aristide.

The Haitian people seemed to respond to his words like an electric charge. I've heard both intellectuals living abroad and starving slumdwellers speak of him with awe. When I ask them why, they have always had the same response: "Father Aristide says aloud in front of everyone what we have the courage to say only among ourselves." Or more simply: "He tells the truth." For years, because of the fear that pervades political life in Haiti, truth has been the rarest of public commodities and truth-sayers the most courageous and admired of men.

Yet it is sometimes difficult to know which comes first, the people or Aristide. The two live in political symbiosis: Aristide listens closely to the murmurings of the people, and responds, and they also listen to what he says, and respond. He admits that he can bring the Haitian people out into the street, but he says he can do so "only when the Haitian people have themselves already decided to take to the street." Yet during difficult days, Haitians from slums like La Saline or Cité Soleil will often refuse to participate in an event unless "Pè Titid" supports it. It is this symbiosis that has allowed Aristide's detractors, among them the Church hierarchy, to assert that he is "leading" his congregation in an unacceptable direction. In fact, no one is leading in this complicated relationship.

In this book, Father Aristide speaks eloquently of the need to overcome Haiti's isolation in the hemisphere. Always referred to as the hemisphere's poorest nation, Haiti has for too long been considered an anomaly by its neighbors in Latin America and the Caribbean. In the 17th century, it was the richest of the colonies; in the 20th, the poorest among the independent nations. Haiti, it is true, has had an exceptional history. The site of the only successful slave revolution in human history, begun in 1791, it became — after a protracted and bloody war, arguably the first war of national liberation — the world's first black republic, declared in 1804. In addition, Haiti can claim the dubious honor of having been the first Third-World debtor nation (in the early 1800s). Certainly, the black republic was a pariah among the world community for more than a century — and remains something of an outcast even today.

In part because of its isolation, Haiti has fallen into all the worst traps of Third-Worldism and dependence: For years it has been controlled by civilian or military dictatorships, its labor grossly exploited, its economy degraded, its political opposition corrupted or silenced. In every walk of life, corruption has become commonplace, and the international drug trade has made the welcoming island one of its pit-stops for cocaine trans-shipment.

Haiti is always portrayed in the darkest of terms; "Impossible to deepen that night," wrote Graham Greene of François Duvalier's regime. But was Dr. Duvalier so very different from the other dictators of Latin America? Was he a worse killer than Pinochet or Stroessner? Has Haiti been a more vicious police state than Guatemala or El Salvador or Argentina or Chile? I know the extent of the brutality in Haiti, and I would say no. Is the disparity in wealth between rich and poor that much wider in Haiti than in other Latin American countries? No. What has been at work in descriptions of Haiti — and its political systems, its religious structures, its social mores — is racism, a racism that was explicit in the decades that followed Haiti's shocking revolution and that in our more decorous days is still understood if unspoken.

There are many reasons why Father Aristide chose to write

In the Parish of the Poor as a letter to his brothers and sisters in the Latin American Church. First, he felt that his country was slowly emerging from its "night," and that given the current political climate, Haiti would need all the support it could get from the rest of the hemisphere, which knows only too well the risks of "transitions to democracy." Second, he felt that it was important to make an international audience aware of the persecutions against the liberation church in Haiti — to add the Haitian chapter to the already voluminous documentation about violence against the progressive clergy and involved lay people in the rest of the hemisphere.

Most of all, however, his habitual urge to bear witness motivated him. As an outcast in an outcast nation, he felt driven to describe what Haiti had become and why, as well as what Haiti might become, if the rest of the world would bear witness with him. Father Aristide writes in his letter about the old ties between Haiti and the rest of Latin America. Not many know that some of Simon Bolivar's expeditions were funded by leaders of the Haitian revolution. This historical connection speaks of an age-old solidarity, one often tarnished by politics and racism, perhaps (even Bolivar eventually betrayed his Haitian benefactors), but nonetheless a foundation upon which to build strong bonds for the future.

In sending this letter to his colleagues in the Church throughout Latin America, Father Aristide reaffirms that bond within a contemporary context. He is asking for support, for protection. For in *In the Parish of the Poor*, not only does he inform his colleagues of the long and bitter story of Haiti's recent history, but by publishing it, by letting his colleagues know what has happened and what may happen again, he defends from their own worst enemies those who have fought and are fighting for change in Haiti. Their worst enemies, Father Aristide often points out, are not soldiers, or Duvalierists, or the Tontons Macoute, but rather the ignorance and abandonment of friends and neighbors.

In the Parish of the Poor, then, is a letter to friends and neighbors from someone with an unhappy story to tell. It is a story that friends and neighbors should know, a cautionary tale, and one whose plot, as Father Aristide notes, will not be entirely new to other activists in the hemisphere. But the intensity of Father Aristide's words and the vigor of his belief and optimism give us hope that his is not a story fated to be relived, that Haiti is not a country doomed to darkness and damnation, and that ours is not a hemisphere condemned to eternal oppression. In these ambiguous times, Father Aristide's courage, his conviction, and the purity of his voice are rare and needed gifts.

—AMY WILENTZ

❧ PART I ❧

IN THE PARISH
OF THE POOR

MAGGIE STEBER

A Letter to My Brothers and Sisters

To All My Sisters and Brothers who have worked for so
long in the parishes of the poor, in the campos and in the
barrios of our common hemisphere —

To All My Sisters and Brothers who have struggled for the
liberation of our peoples in the name of Jesus Christ against
the heaviest of odds — against the intransigent forces of guns
and of miters and of money —

To All My Tireless Sisters and Brothers who have
labored and spoken out against the abuses of a cruel system,
taking every risk a woman or a man can take in this short life
granted to us —

Greetings

In a dark corner of our little world, I take up my pen to write
to you. The light I set by my side to illuminate my task is a faint
light, but an unwavering one. It will grow stronger as I write,
because it is the light of solidarity, and as you read this letter,
too, that same light that is by your side will grow in intensity,
because the light of solidarity is the one beacon that we the
oppressed have to light our way through the dark corners and
byways of our little world. If we hold that torch ahead of us, we
will never stray from our path, though our road is long and weary
and filled with obstacles: barricades, bullets, ambush, fire, and
death.

I live in Haiti.

The other day in the midst of Port-au-Prince, the great

degraded capital city that is my home, I saw a car, an old bat-
tered car, a jalopy, falter and sputter and come to a slow halt.
It was out of gas; this happens often in my destitute country,
where everyone and everything is so poor that the donkeys and
horses are starving and even the cars must try to get by on
nothing. The man who was driving the car got out and looked
at it, stuck there in the middle of traffic, helpless. Then I saw
another face, the passenger. A woman. She looked out of the
back window with tears in her eyes, and the driver looked
around the street at the unemployed loungers who are always
there, and said to them, "She is going to have a baby right here."
He told them that he had taken the woman from her home
because the midwife was unable to help her. The pregnancy was
difficult, and the woman needed to go to the hospital to have
her baby. Now the tears were coming down the woman's cheeks.
"If we do not get to the hospital, she will die," the man told the
loungers. "Her baby will die, too."

The loungers—hungry young men who had never had a job
and who never will have a job if my country goes on as it has
done for the last half century—looked at the car and heard the
man's voice and saw the woman's tears. Their backs straight-
ened, their cigarettes fell to the ground, their eyes cleared. They
approached the car, eight of them, leaned over, and put their
shoulders to the chore. The driver steered. The woman lay back.
Down one long dusty road, a left turn, and down another,
through the green and white gates of the State Hospital, and
she had arrived.

That was the force of solidarity at work, a recognition that
we are all striving toward the same goal, and that goal is to go
forward, to advance, to bring into this world another way of
being. Even if the motor has died, even if the engine is out of
gas, that new way of being can be brought into this world through
solidarity. The loungers are an awakened populace, the driver
brings them the words to awaken them, and the woman carries
within her, on her seat in the old beat-up car, the new life, the
new Haiti.

(In my story—the story that has been given to me to live as
my life and to tell to you—there is another woman who suffered

in childbirth. She suffered wounds and lacerations in order to bring forth another child who also represents the new Haiti, and that child is called Hope, she is called Esperancia. But that story, the story of Hope, is for a later part of my letter to you, dear sisters, dear brothers.)

That other baby—the one who was born in the State Hospital that afternoon—lived because Haitians worked together in solidarity. But alone, as you well know, none of the southern nations that exist—or that subsist—in the deepening shadow of that greater state to our north can deliver a new world. In Haiti, alone together, we are only some six million strong. That is not enough, not alone. But with our brothers and sisters across the water, in Mexico, in El Salvador and Guatemala, in Belize, in Nicaragua and Honduras, in Costa Rica, in Panama, in Colombia and Venezuela, in Brazil, in Ecuador and Guyana and Suriname and French Guiana, in Peru, Bolivia, Paraguay, Uraguay, and in Argentina, in Chile, in all the southern nations teetering upon the brink of change—with their help, with the help of tens of millions more: *Venceremos*. We shall overcome.

Let us speak one another's languages, the languages of slaves and of indigenous peoples as well as the languages of our colonizers. *Nous vaincrons*. We shall overcome. It is time to organize. *Formez vos bataillons*. Let us form battalions, in the words of the French revolutionary song. Let us continue to work together, throughout the hemisphere, as we have already begun to do. God, as the British military saying goes, is for the big battalions. Let that be our motto, also. In Creole we say: *Ansanm, ansanm, jis nou genyen batay-la*. Together unto victory. God is for the big battalions. Let the new children of the hemisphere be born. Let us all join in solidarity to hasten their delivery with words and acts of deliverance.

Where is Haiti? To many of you who live on that almost continuous land mass that stretches from the Rio Grande to Tierra del Fuego, my country remains a mystery. Haiti is a small and crowded nation, six million souls living on 27,500 square kilometers of land. We are removed from you by water and by history. But we are also bound to you by water and by history. Port-au-Prince is where you are, just as Recife is where I am, and so is Lima, so is Santiago, so is Panama City, so is San Salvador. Medellín 1968 is where we are. We should not be mysteries to one another.

Brothers and sisters, I want to lift the veil of mystery that hides my true country from your eyes. Let me guide you through those dark corners and byways of Haiti so that together we can get to a place where there is light. The way is long, but we have come a long way already. Together, we will get there. For now, let me be your guide. Later, you will be mine.

I speak to you of dark corners and byways, and you think perhaps that I am speaking in metaphor. Or perhaps you reflect on the dark byways of your own countries, and then you know that what I am talking about is real.

The dark places I know best are my country's slums. The church where I used to preach sat on the edges of one of these, La Saline, and in the old days, before it became impossible, I used to walk through La Saline and the other slums like it that are spreading like contagion in a city that for years has been clogged with the detritus of the deadly economic infection called capitalism. In La Saline, there are many dark byways, paths that run between two rows of shanties made of plywood and cardboard and old, disintegrating tin. One bright hot day I walked down one of these corridors, a dark byway even in the hot Haitian sun, and at the end I found a courtyard with three naked children, my country's new generation, bathing in a puddle of garbage left from the rains of the night before. On another day, I walked down another corridor in the darkness of our bright sun, and at the end I found a wider road, and three young boys in tattered shorts, playing marbles in the dirt. The new generation. On another day, I walked down another corridor and three young girls — wearing secondhand dresses thrown away by nice middle-class girls in a northern country and brought here by profiteering middlemen — these young girls were selling themselves for quarters and dimes and less to any man, and that was the new generation of my beloved country.

There was another dark corridor I used to see when I traveled around my city, this one also in bright sunlight, in a better part of town. Every morning you could see this dark corridor form. It was a line, a line that formed every morning before dawn. Where did it form, this sad, dark line? Outside the consulate of that big northern country that casts so many long, dark shadows in our hemisphere. This was the visa line, a long, dispirited dog's tail of a line. Each person carried in his hand a large envelope with an X-ray of his lungs inside. All these Haitians — my generation, these — are trying to leave our beloved country, and why? Because they see no future here, no promise, no way to live. And yet these people — who have the money for a visa and a ticket for an airplane and a place to live in that great, cold northern country — are the best educated of Haiti's small middle and lower-middle class, our artisans, our engineers, our schoolteachers, our shopkeepers, our nurses and our students. All of them standing there, in front of that great white consulate, ready to show their lungs to some cold official who is empowered to grant or not to grant them the right — the right! — to leave Haiti for the land of snow. And this, because the land of snow has exploited my beloved country to such an extent that there is too little left here — in what used to be called paradise — to give my people comfort. And so those who seek even a minimum of comfort, not just for themselves but for the family they are leaving behind in Haiti, must depart.

Those who are not so fortunate as to know a doctor who will take a picture of their lungs, to know a consular officer who might look on their case kindly, to have the money to buy a ticket for Miami or New York — they leave on boats, little boats overflowing with my country's poor, mothers with babies at their breasts, young men who cannot read, peasants whose only skill is with the hoe or with the sail and the fisherman's net. They never get where they are going, my brave countrymen. If they do not drown in high winds and high waters, they are turned back at sea by the thousands — at first, every year, but now, every month, by the thousands. The men who turn them back are agents of that same cold country that refuses visas to those whose lives it has ruined: the United States, its Coast Guard.

Coast Guard cutter: that is the name of the boat those agents pilot, but those words sound to us in Haiti today like a new description of Death with his sweeping scythe. When my countrymen are returned to their native soil by the Coast Guard cutter, they huddle on the dock, penniless, no way to return home, often no home to return to, all their savings gone into the aborted voyage to mythical Miami. This is my generation, the mothers and fathers of Haiti's new generation. My generation is running away from Haiti, with its dark corners and byways. I want to call them back before they begin their fruitless travels.

But what will they come back to? Where will they remain? I say to them: Come back and make a new Haiti. Spurn comfort. Come back, live in misery, and build a new way. Of all people, you—brothers and sisters—know what it means to build a new way when everyone who is working on the new construction is living in misery. You have seen the people scavenging for food on the garbage heaps of Rio de Janeiro, and you have seen them starving in the barrios of Panama City. You know how hard it is to build Utopia on a garbage heap; indeed, it is hard to build even a decent poor man's home there. But that is all we ask, a decent poor man's home, and no more corruption, no more inflicted misery, no more children bathing in sewage.

That is what I ask my people to come back to build. It is not so very much, a decent poor man's home—not such a big job. But in my country, and in your countries, it seems impossible. That is because we are all living under a system so corrupt that to ask for a plate of rice and beans every day for every man, woman and child is to preach a revolution. That is the crime of which I stand accused: preaching food for all men and women.

I have spoken of—and indeed, I can imagine—a Haiti where at three or four in the afternoon, every afternoon, every person sits down and has a great big steaming hot plate of rice and beans. That would be a peaceful country. Today, the country is not peaceful. In some places, the people hardly manage to eat one hot meal a week. In other dark places throughout the country, men and women work all day in their dry fields and have only a few plantains for dinner. They crouch and eat with their fingers, because they cannot afford a fork. In dark places in the provincial towns, they travel all morning to market and then sit there all day selling their wares and earning only a few pennies, and then they have only a few plantains to eat for dinner, or a bit of cassava, or rice without beans, or a little cornmeal.

Yet while the peasant eats his cornmeal mash with his fingers, men and women up on a hill high above my dying Port-au-Prince are sitting at tables and eating steaks and pâté and veal flown in from across the water. The rich of my country, a tiny percentage of our population, sit at a vast table covered in white damask and overflowing with good food, while the rest of my countrymen and countrywomen are crowded under that table, hunched over in the dirt and starving. It is a violent situation, and one day the people under that table will rise up in righteousness, and knock the table of privilege over, and take what rightfully belongs to them. Brothers and sisters, it is our mission to help them stand up and live as human beings. That is what we have all been working for for all these years in the parishes of the poor.

I have written to you of dark corridors and visa lines and lines of boats heading away from Haitian shores. Now let me speak to you of another kind of line, one we have seen in Haiti recently, as have you who live in El Salvador, in Chile, in Panama. This is the voting line. On November 29, 1987, these voting lines were scrawled across every parish in my country like a message of hope. And then? And then, nothing. Or worse than nothing. Do you remember? Did news of what happened to our voting lines reach you across the water?

Along with the agents of the United States, our government — a military dictatorship then as now — encouraged the Haitian people to stand in line to vote. And the Haitian people came, mothers, grandmothers, fathers, uncles, daughters, whole families lined up. The forces of order wanted us to vote so that it would appear to the outside world that we were a happy, peaceful democracy, and then the exploitation and corruption could

MAGGIE STEBER

go on just as before. But even that hypocritical experiment in what the northern countries call democracy was too much for our Haitian authorities. On our first election day—I hope that you recall that election day—the Haitian Army (which is the government) and its accomplices came and massacred the voters as they waited for their turn to elect a president.

Soon after this experience of death and "democracy," we had another election, also encouraged by the military dictatorship and the United States. This time the voters on those lines were paid agents of the dictatorship, and the man they "elected" was a puppet, a president with whom the United States said it could cooperate. But again, the Haitian authorities couldn't stand the change, and again the military marched in, this time to depose its own marionette.

Every day in those dark times, we asked ourselves what is democracy, if people are starving? How can you trust a vote when a man will vote for whomever gives him the money to feed his children that night? Starving men will vote in exchange for a plate of rice or a glass of rum or a can of concentrated milk.

For a bottle of rum and seven dollars, they will do much worse things. But that, like the story of the child called Hope, is for a later part of my letter to you. You must know the beginnings of the story before you can understand its end. You must learn the language before you can understand the message. You must pry the deepest roots of the tree away from the hard earth before you can pull it up.

I live in Haiti.

Listen to the beginnings of our story. Haitian history has never been easy. We were a nation of slaves who rose up against the colonizers and made a revolution. In 1804 we severed our ties to France and ended the exploitation of black slaves by white masters. The Haitian slaves set the course for the liberation of all Latin America. Indeed, the Liberator himself, Simon Bolivar, twice received arms and sustenance from our third free leader, Alexandre Pétion, after Bolivar had been banished from Venezuela. In 1815 Pétion provided Bolivar with gunpowder, guns, and a printing press to spread words and encourage acts of deliverance. In 1816 Pétion equipped Bolivar once again. In return for that support, Pétion asked Bolivar to free slaves wherever he routed the Spanish. Bolivar, in recognition of Haiti's help, gave Pétion a massive ceremonial sword, although he did not always keep faith with his Haitian friends.

While Haiti was supporting liberation throughout Latin America, at home corruption and greed conspired to oppress free Haitians just as those twin evils had our slave forbears. Does this sound all too familiar to your ears, brothers and sisters? Black masters with ties to white empires proved as heartless in Haiti as had their earlier white counterparts. Has not this happened in all of our nations? Our leaders gain freedom only to turn around and oppress the peoples who supported them. What nation among us has had an unblemished history since gaining independence? And in today's modern world, things are hardly better. Let us not talk only of Haiti's shameful Duvalier, but of Somoza, Peron, Pinochet, Stroessner, of D'Aubuisson's ARENA in El Salvador. These men were or are not unique in their nations' histories, but simply represent the latest in a long line of dictators, products of the old colonial imperialist ways.

Together, like Petion and Bolivar, you and I and all of our brothers and sisters in Latin America can do something to ensure that Somoza and Peron and Pinochet and Stroessner will turn out to be the last generation in that long line of *caudillos*. It will not be easy. Even when the *caudillo* is gone, he is still with us. Today in Haiti we have Duvalierism without Duvalier; in Argentina, you have Peronism without Peron; in Nicaragua, the Somocistas are still plotting to return to power; in Salvador, ARENA is already at the helm.

It is time to put Bolivar's shining sword — a sword whose blade extends from our shores to your shores — to good use. Only at great peril do we lose sight of our peoples' historic connections, our shared birthright. If we lose those memories we will be like the old sick man who does not recognize his friends and brothers when they visit, and who instead, dying, leaves his beautiful inheritance to his enemies. I think of my letter to you as a product of our shared inheritance. This letter is a leaflet from the Liberator's Haitian printing press, encouraging us all to take up Bolivar's fierce sword of liberty. Let us not forget Pétion and Bolivar; let us not waste what little remains of their precious legacy.

Among the dark corners and byways of our common hemisphere, where shall we look for Bolivar's bright sword? I know where, you know where, brothers and sisters. Let us look in the parishes of the poor. Let us look down all those dark corridors through which I have taken you. Let us walk past the children bathing in garbage, past the young half-naked boys and their game of marbles, past the three young girls who are trying to sell us their bodies. Let us walk a little further on. Be careful of the mud. Don't slip. Take my hand.

Night is falling, but I see a light shining over there, in that little shack over there, with its doors closed. Do you see that slice of light shining out from the cracks in the plywood? Let's go inside.

The one room inside the little shack is crowded with young people, and a few who are not so young. It's hot. A young woman standing at the back is directing the discussion. What are those words we hear the people saying? *Libète*. Liberty. *Dwa moun*. Human rights. *Teyoloji liberasyon*. Liberation theology. A pot of hot rice and beans is being distributed, paid for by contributions from everyone present. What is this place, what is this group, why are they gathered here under the light of one bare bulb to talk about liberty? You know what this is, brothers and sisters, as well as I do. This is an ecclesial base community; in Haiti, we call them *ti kominote legliz*. Today, you can find groups like this all over Latin America; there are more than 300,000 of them in our hemisphere. I work with them, brothers and sisters, and so do you.

Today in Haiti, as in many of your countries, these little enlightened communities are in danger—from the state and from elements of the hierarchy of our Church. The story I have been given to tell you is the story of how those huge forces have combined in my country to attack the base communities; my story, the story of my life, is that story. In Haiti, those communities have been threatened, attacked, burned, beaten, shot and slashed, but they are still defiant, still working and talking together, trying to build a decent poor man's house upon our great garbage heap.

Let's leave them to their rice and beans, hoping that tonight is another night when they will work and eat in peace, and not a night when the soldiers will burst in and arrest them, or open fire.

I want to take you back to the markets in the countryside. Night is falling, and the women have put their baskets on their heads and are beginning the long walk home to their little villages where if they are lucky they will eat some plantain soup with their children before they go to sleep. But what is that light in that small hut over there? Do you see a slice of light peeking through a crack near the door of that mud hut? Let's go inside.

Inside it is hot and crowded. A lantern is lit in one corner; in another burns a candle. Who are these men with their rough hands and their rusty machetes? Who are these women with their market baskets on their laps? What are those words we catch, words that they say in whispers for fear that the Army's people are spying on them? *Libète*. Liberty. *Dwa moun*. Human rights. *Dwa abitan*. Peasants' rights. *Refòm agrè*. Land reform. You know who these people are, brothers and sisters, as well as I do. This is a peasants' work group. Every day, they work together in the fields and try to use their unified labor to stop the big landholders' exploitation of the peasants. Sometimes they succeed, but sometimes they fail and are punished by the forces of order. The story I have been given to tell you is the story of how those forces of order have combined in my country to attack the peasants' work groups. My story, the story of my life, is that story. In Haiti, those work groups have been threatened, attacked, run out of their homes, beaten, slashed, and massacred. But they are still defiant, still working and talking together, trying to plant a decent poor man's field upon our great garbage heap. For all these years we have been working with them too, brothers and sisters.

Look at their machetes. The blades are rusted, the handles dirty. The peasants let the knives hang at their sides except when they are working in the field. But don't be fooled. A machete is useful in almost any situation. Those rusty blades are long and sharp. They remind me of Bolivar's sword.

In my country there are other dimly lit rooms where people are meeting to organize for a new way of life. There are youth groups and women's groups and associations of the unemployed. There are unions and journalists' organizations. There are human rights groups, professional confederations, and neighborhood vigilance brigades.

Once, during a time of troubles when my country's government was particularly vicious—when base communities throughout the country were under physical attack and more than two hundred members of a large peasant movement in Jean-Rabel in our northwest province had been massacred—I spoke to the people of these groups, spoke to all my countrymen and countrywomen in the four dark corners of my nation. I spoke Jesus' words then, and now they, too, remind me of Bolivar's blade.

"And he that hath no sword," I quoted, "let him sell his garment, and buy one" (Luke 22:36). With these words from the Gospels, I was urging my countrymen to defend themselves against the onslaught of the military and the paramilitary forces in Haiti; I was urging them to defend themselves against the diabolical, Machiavellian, satanic forces that were gathering against them, against the forces that were massing to extinguish what few little lights of solidarity we had managed to keep burning over the years.

The government—that is to say, the military and the paramilitary forces—did not take kindly to Jesus' words. The Minister of Information said that I was preaching armed struggle, and the campaign against me and against all those who worked with me, against the ecclesial base communities, against the peasant movements, against the vigilance brigades, and against so many comrades I did not know but who were on our side, grew more vicious, more violent.

More than two hundred had already died, and scores more would be martyred as the movement continued. Like all of you, brothers and sisters, I have lost friends in this long and bitter struggle. The blood of those beloved martyrs only makes the fight more valiant, and the distant goal sweeter. For their sakes, we must not lose sight of the path of liberation that we can cut through the jungle, with solidarity's sword.

Let me tell you my story. I will try to be brief, although it is a long story, a sad story whose ending is still unwritten. It is a story of speaking, and believing, of a perilous voyage with death along the way, and of a great assembly, and a massacre. It is a story of exile and of disobedience. Most of all, it is the story not of one man, but of a people, my people. It is a story about our will to survive, and our survival, but it is also the story of the forces that are ranged against us, the forces of military might and foreign exploitation and huge sums of capital amassed.

My story is a story of light and of shadow. The light is the light of solidarity, and that little light, growing stronger in spite of dark clouds that threaten it, shines through the clouds and illuminates so many of my struggling brothers and sisters, and also, if you look hard, so many evildoers. My brothers and sisters stand tall in that light: they are not afraid. But the evildoers run and hide, they hide in the shadows, hoping darkness will protect them and allow them cover to continue committing their crimes, their massacres, to continue to enforce their repression.

With the light of solidarity—which is the light of life—shining upon them (shining from them, really), my brothers and sisters are sadly watching the evildoers go about their unclean business. But my brothers and sisters are unafraid, their courage does not weaken in the face of savagery. Rather, their courage grows greater and greater, as they look harder and harder—in the light of life—for means to combat the shadows, to illuminate the dark corners, to bring light into the regions of obscurity. Holding in their hands the light of solidarity, the light of justice, the light of liberty, the light of dignity, the light of respect, like flashlights of life flickering along a midnight country road, my struggling brothers and sisters are looking for the path that leads to the secret that will allow them to disperse the shadows where the evildoers are hiding, waiting to do more evil.

My story, and the story of my struggling Haitian brothers and sisters, is the story of your people, too, brothers and sisters. Listen, and then tell me you do not recognize yourselves, your brethren and—yes—your enemies, too, your evildoers, all of them characters in the story that is my life, that is your lives. All of them living in a land where there is darkness and shadow—but light also.

The crime of which I stand accused is the crime of preaching food for all men and women. According to the authorities in my country and in Rome, this is tantamount to preaching revolution, war. But what war? I ask.

History has proven that some wars are just. This war I have been accused of advocating is an avoidable war, one that I and all men and women who care for peace and the well-being of our parishioners would wish to avoid. The men eating at the great table could avoid it if they wished to, and merely by the simple fraternal act of sharing: sharing wealth, sharing power, breaking bread with their brothers and sisters. But these men, among them bishops, do not wish for the well-being of their parishioners; they wish rather for their own well-being, and the well-being of those who sit at the great table. They remind me of the Pharisees who make clean the outside of the cup and the platter but their inward part is full of ravening and wickedness (Luke 11:39). If they do not wish to share fraternally with those whom, before the world, they call brother and sister, then they must accept the fate that they have chosen. They must accept the simple fact that it is they, and not I and my colleagues, who are advocating war.

I have participated in many struggles in my life, but none has pained me so greatly as the struggle within our Church over the depth of that Church's preferential option for the poor of our parish. There are those of us, usually younger and eager for change, who believe that that commitment should be total, unrelenting, intransigent. There are others, often with grayer heads and more comfortable with the ways of the world, who do not mind conciliating the powers that sit around the great table, who believe that collaboration and compromise are a valid means in taking up our preferential option for the poor. In my heart I am sure that the way of total commitment is the right way, but perhaps time and life will change me, as they have so many others. I doubt it.

I fear often that those in the hierarchy of the Church who believe in compromise are willing to compromise in one direction only, and that is with power. They do not want to compromise with those of us in the Church who have a different vision of the Church's role. Often, when we of the Little Church—Ti Legliz, as the liberation church is called in Haiti—are engaged in a struggle and need the counsel of our older brothers in the hierarchy, they refuse to meet us, to speak with us. This causes discord, and discord is not good for the Church or for Haiti.

Often, we fear that the cold behavior of our older brothers is dictated by another man, a man who lives in another country, a country not his own, a man who wears long white robes, and stands, an equal, beside the Church's beloved yellow and white banner. You know which man I mean, brothers and sisters.

That man in Rome is our brother in Jesus Christ. He is a brother to the poor of Haiti, and to those of us in the Little Church. I wish him well in his life, and in his sacred mission. I wish him well and honor him and love him as I love all my fellow men and women. But he does not love me in return, brothers and sisters, and we all know that love comes closest to achieving its ideal—which is Jesus' love for his Church and his Church's love for Jesus—when it is requited.

Now, the question I have puzzled over, as I have tried to lead my life over the past three years, has been, Why does this man not love me? Why does he not cherish and protect me as I would do him? Why does he wish to exile me from the loving heart of our sacred family, the Church? How can my brother not love

MEV PULEO

me, when I love him so purely and so passionately, as I do my family, our Church?

Because I have suffered so much for so long in order to keep that profound love pure, I cry out now like a rejected lover. I suffer now the deep pangs of unrequited love. This is a private pain, the pain of the son banished from his mother's hearth. I may speak more of it later, but for me, it is not an easy subject to put my pen to. Let it pass.

Rather than look at me, let us look at him, my brother who would wish to banish me from his community. Let us turn the fine light of our little lamp of solidarity his way. Let us examine his face. It is a kind, fatherly face, but let us see the man for what he truly is. Often, this is a hard task. Can we see our mother for what she is, as the world sees her? Can we see our darling brother, our sweet son, our laughing daughter clearly, as others might see them? When we love, our sight is obscured by affection. We need the pure light of our little lamp to help us see the objects of our love.

Let me turn that light on the face of the man who lives in Rome, my beloved brother. Who is this man, in truth? What is my family, the family he heads, the Church, in truth? Let us be honest, let us be clear-minded. Yes, the Church is by tradition the family of God, and this man is its appointed and anointed leader. That is one truth, one part of the truth. Yes, this man is chosen by his colleagues and then blessed and anointed as infallible. That, too, is one part of the truth. Yes, his word and the word of his bishops becomes a vital part of the doctrine of the Church. That is true. From him at the center extend all powers within the Church throughout the world; that is true. Yet, I must remind myself, and my little lamp helps me remember, he is just a man, a man doing a job.

Ah, my little lamp. Its light of solidarity illuminates the darkest corners of all difficult questions. Just a man doing a job. Now I can see him more clearly. What is the paradigm for the pope in the secular world today? I ask myself. Why, it's all too clear. Of course. All the shadows around him, the smoke and mirrors, fall away. Who is this man? He is the chief executive officer of a multinational corporation. And what is the job of a

chief executive officer of a multinational corporation? To protect the international interests of the company, to ensure its
continued existence, to safeguard its officers from dissension
among its rank-and-file employees and shareholders, and to provide, at the farthest reach of the corporation, a product that the
consumer will purchase. His job is to ensure efficiency, conti-
nuity, and profit, while maintaining the status quo within the
company. I think this is a fair job description for the man who
lives in Rome, and I am not the only one who thinks so. Yet he
and his colleagues have a secret weapon that no other corporate
officers can boast; United Fruit never had this weapon, nor did
Gulf + Western or the National City Bank. That weapon is
belief, the long-established belief of the people – the final consumer – in the word of the Church. The man in Rome and his
colleagues are able to wrap company policy up in the proud
yellow and white of the Church. They can pronounce and pret-
tify efficiency actions using the beautiful words of the Bible.
They can dress up their officers and parade them around the
Church as men of God. They can take the policies of United
Fruit, Gulf + Western and the National City Bank, all multinational corporations like the Church – with the same interests – and package them along with their own policies, and call
that package truth.

But *caveat emptor*! Will the people buy that package? Not
any longer. The various struggles of the world's poor for economic and political liberation, combined with the establishment
of an indigenous clergy and involved lay people (the Little
Church – you, my brothers and sisters!), have made the people
wary of the yellow and white package.

And in truth we ourselves must be careful. We in the Little
Church must negotiate a path between company policy and that
road we know to be the just and honest way, the way of the
Gospels. We must not be swayed to collaborate and conciliate,
but must stay firmly in the camp of the poor. Yet our home is
in the Church. If we do not like what we see in the Church,
we must work to change that, work in the ways we see fit. We
must make sure to build that decent, poor man's home – our
Church – in the parish of the poor, for that is its only proper

neighborhood. Yes, we must be the workers, the slum-dwellers, the peasants, the market women, the street children of the Church. We must work from dawn till dawn to make our home brighter, cleaner, more blessed.

We must never become foremen and middle managers and assistant CEOs and deputy administrators. Because middle management can never be trusted with the fate of the workers. That is what has happened in Haiti—most of the middle management and executives of the Church have not simply walked away from the workers, but have striven actively to impede the workers' progress toward liberty and equality.

The list of their mistakes is long and unfortunate.

Too often, members of the hierarchy have preached against the movement of the people. At ill-chosen moments thay have advised putting the brakes on the Haitian people, who were ready to risk their lives to rid the nation of all the old criminals and all the old, corrupt ways. This has meant that today, the old criminals and old ways are still in force.

When it became clear that the Church's literacy program was finally having some effect, the bishops shut it down, thus ensuring that their flock would continue on in unlettered ignorance.

The bishops supported the sham elections that ended in blood for the hapless Haitian voter.

They supported the puppet president who was later selected by the Army, and who was deposed four months after his selection.

They spoke as one against the Little Church, accusing us of every kind of sin against our Church and our pope and our nation.

They attempted to silence me, to send me away, to banish me.

They silenced many among my brothers, or sent them away.

They waited weeks to speak out against the carnage that took place when death crossed my doorstep.

They dismissed all of the journalists who gave the Church's radio station in Haiti its legitimacy and popularity.

Thus, they have effectively closed the Church's own mouth in Haiti—they have tried to close my mouth, the mouths of my brothers and sisters in the Church, and the mouths of their own employees, the committed journalists of Radio Soleil. Today, the Church in Haiti, once filled with hymns and hope, is silent.

Ah, but I was going to tell you my story. You see how I shy away from it? I avoid it, I try to forget it, to put it behind me. But the story—like all stories of blood and betrayal—is unforgettable and must be told. Everywhere we turn in Haiti today, this story rises up in the collective gorge and begs to be uttered. I would wish that another would tell it to you for me, but almost all of those who know the truth are silent. The story has too much meaning, it is too powerful, they are afraid that it will ignite upon their lips, beneath their pens. They too shy away from it, and so it is left to me, brothers and sisters, to summon up my energies and tell the long, hard tale.

I go over it again and again, in my head. I see it as a road of darkness, a long highway of gloom that my friends and colleagues and I have traveled. I like to think that we journeyed down this unending highway in the night and shadows in hazardous conditions in order to arrive somewhere special, in order to arrive at the horizon, at sunrise. I like to think that by telling the tale, I will encourage that sun to rise, I will hasten the day. I bow my head and hope that I am right.

Let me begin with guns. In Haiti, guns are often at the vortex of current events. Does this sound like your countries, brothers? sisters? I know it does. This is the story of guns. (Notice, as you read, that it is always the wrong men who have the guns. This is one of the lessons that the men with guns taught me.)

For a long time, I used to say Mass at nine o'clock on Sundays in my small, pleasant church at the edge of the slum in our degraded capital. It was hot, but we were happy. Happy to be together, sitting down, talking, in the shadow of the high roof of St. Jean Bosco, for that hour—and not apart, competing for pennies in the slum's crowded market, standing each man and woman alone, unshaded. Those were our hours of peace, for me, for my congregation, hours of peace in the parish of the

poor. I talked with them about many things during those sermons, but of all the lessons I tried to impart to them, every
Sunday, and of all the lessons they taught me, I think the most
important was to shun death, and embrace life. To shun the
ways of death, and embrace the ways of life. To run from the
evildoers' darkness, and toward the light of life. That is, to move
always toward freedom, away from slavery. This is a lesson we
Haitians understand, because of our history.

St. Jean Bosco was a place of light and life, and laughter and
music, too. There are not too many places like that in my country. It was special, safe, welcoming. It was open to all men and
women. I preached to that congregation, the congregation of all
men and women, and so did the lay workers of my church, young
men and women committed to light and to life. My church was
a place where anyone—market woman, beggar, jobless young
man, student, child, anyone—could speak out to the congregation. I loved that place.

But because my church was open to all, it was sometimes a
dangerous place. The shadowy evildoers could not countenance
all the light that poured out from my little church. They did not
want Haitians to be able to meet freely and discuss their
problems. They did not want Haitians to hear their brothers and
sisters analyze the political situation. They did not like the idea
that such a place existed. They wanted to put an end to it, to
shut out the light, stop the music, turn the laughter to tears. Of
course, there was no way to do that but with a gun. You can
only stop life by killing it.

The first time—for there is always a first time, but never a
last—was years ago, although to me, it seems recent (all such
events play before my eyes like an endless film). It took place
in the last days of the dictator, and I will name him, since we
have had so many dictators, before this one and after him as
well. Jean-Claude Duvalier was about to fall. The Haitian people in the provinces had risen against him—and some of them
had fallen, too, in that brave struggle. But Port-au-Prince, the
dark capital of my country, had not yet spoken out, had not yet
taken to the streets, though in corners here and there around
the city, people were talking about what to do, were deliberating

about the next action. My church was one of those bright corners. We had been meeting for several weeks to try and organize a demonstration, not a demonstration for a demonstration's sake, but a demonstration to demonstrate our solidarity, our sincerity, our honesty, and our sympathy with the rest of the country. To say: We are on your side. To say, in the words of Martin Luther King, another of our brothers: We shall overcome.

Duvalier had imposed a state of siege. It was a confused time: some thought he had already left the country, others believed he was still in Haiti. The confusion, spread by rumormongers in Haiti and in the cold dark country to the north, made it more difficult to organize against Duvalier, since we weren't sure that he was still there to organize against. When the state of siege was announced (it was a Sunday in January 1986), there was a meeting in the courtyard of my church. People were afraid, it is true, but in the end, they decided that, state of siege or not, the demonstration had already been planned, and it would take place. That it would not be a political demonstration, but a demonstration of faith, of integrity. In fact, the demonstration began as a demonstration of faith, but in the end, it became a political demonstration.

That morning, before the demonstration was to take place, I was to say my usual nine o'clock Sunday morning Mass. But before that, I heard a noise coming from the church, and they came to find me. I went into the sacristy and I saw through the grating that the courtyard in front was full of people holding tree branches in their hands—in Haiti, a sign of a crowd ready to demonstrate. I hurried into the church, where two priests were saying the early morning Mass. I sat down on a chair near them, and I could hear the people inside and outside chanting: "Miracle, miracle," and waving the branches above their heads. "Miracle, miracle," they chanted. "Long live St. Jean Bosco." There was a sort of panic of excitement inside the church, and I was wondering if I would be able to rise to the situation and calm the crowd, when suddenly I saw a man appear before me with a revolver trained on me. I didn't know if he was going to shoot me, or what he was going to do with it. But the way I felt about it then—as I still do, years after—was that because of my temperament, my conviction, my faith, my duty and my responsibility, if I were to die, let me die in my place, where I belong. Therefore I just sat there, waiting, and he pointed the revolver at me, and then—miracle, miracle—he opened it, took out the bullets, and handed the gun and the bullets to me.

The day followed the course it was destined to follow. The people did demonstrate, the Army did come, there was a standoff. Above all else, Port-au-Prince had finally spoken. The dictator fell a week later. As for the man with the gun, this is what I heard about him. (I do not know if it is true.) He had the gun, and a small basket. In the basket was a photograph of me, a lot of money, and a passport. The photograph was to show him his target, the money was to pay him for the assassination, and the passport was to get him out of the country. I heard that for his pains, he received a beating from the congregation. I handed the gun and the bullets over to a bishop. That was the end of that, for the moment. The day of my death had come and had gone, and I was still alive. My congregation counted me lucky. They counted me blessed. But as I have said, there is always a first time, but never a last. The story of the struggle—at its climax—is always about guns.

The Haitian people had chased their dictator out of the country, a sweet victory, but—as we always knew—only one move in a very long and violent game. We had taken the king and queen, but this was an odd game of chess, a modern game of chess, and thus, still on the board, the bishops and the knights in their safe castles, and all their little pawns, went on playing out the long and violent game. On our side, we never had had king, queen, bishops, knights or castles. We played with the most ignoble of the pieces, the little fellows in the front line, and we were winning, or so it seemed, and we went on playing, too. Their king and queen had been knocked off, but the confrontation continued. On our side, it was the spirit of the Haitian people that moved the small, humble pieces across the board. On their side, the cold country to our north and the man in Rome were dictating strategy.

Immediately, they replaced their Haitian king. The new one came in the guise of a knight — a soldier, a general, in fact — and he, like Duvalier, was happy to array his pieces in such a way as to stop the forward movement of the people. He never disarmed Duvalier's secret police, the nightmare Tontons Macoute. He never tried to change the corrupt system of economic abuse and exploitation that has wrecked our country and the lives of all our people. He loved power and money, authority. He never loved democracy. He was the enemy of the people, although he came to power at a moment where it seemed as though he might be a white knight bearing good news, helping to rescue the distraught people from its misery and enslavement. But he never moved an inch in our favor, on our behalf. He worked against us, and kept his little feet in their black army boots planted firmly in the people's path, with his Uzi trained upon us.

It did not take us long to recognize that this new president was just a new actor in an old role. All we had to do was look down the snout of his Uzi, and there, in that deep dark recess, we could see Duvalier's face. Still, we kept advancing.

On April 26, not even three months after Duvalier had fled before the people's wrath, the people decided to commemorate the victims of one of the darkest places in all of Haiti, Fort Dimanche. The light of life does not shine on Fort Dimanche. Just down the road from my little church, this notorious prison sat like a black hole, sucking up what pieces of life were thrown into its swallowing gorge. During the years of its use as a prison and torture camp, it grew bigger and bigger, fattening itself on the blood of the Haitian people. Its excesses of cruelty left the entire nation in mourning. Its claws reached into the bosoms of thousands of families, snatching away sons, daughters, fathers, mothers, sisters, brothers, newlyweds, and children, never to be seen again. It was a symbol of the Army and the police and the Tontons Macoute, of all the forces organized to destroy us.

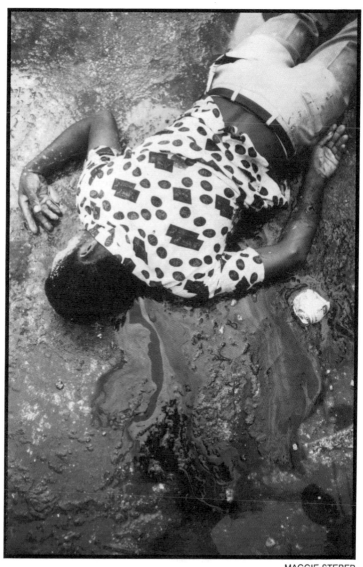

MAGGIE STEBER

It was decided that a Mass of mourning would be said at Sacre Coeur Church, and then a procession would wind through town to Fort Dimanche, where we would kneel and pray for the prison's victims. I rode alongside the procession with another priest and a few journalists from the Church radio station, Radio Soleil, in the station's jeep. (In French, *soleil* means "sun", the light of life.) We were broadcasting live from the procession, and we would broadcast live from Fort Dimanche. We arrived at the prison in the midst of a crowd of thousands and thousands of people, people who were suffering because they remembered their children, the families they had lost, they were swimming in pain, they were enveloped in the blackness of mourning because too many bad memories had turned into a long nightmare before their eyes.

We had just arrived in front of the prison when shots rang out, shot after shot. Everyone began to run. People lost their shoes. Tear gas fell upon us. It was so horrifying that we had to ask ourselves whether what we were seeing could possibly be true. It was so odd, so shocking, that even when we saw what was happening before our very eyes, we could not believe it was happening. But we could not lie to ourselves; we kept our eyes open to make sure it was not a hallucination of the past we were witnessing, to make sure that this new nightmare was real. The head of Fort Dimanche was there, lying flat on his stomach, with his gun in his hand as if he were hunting. They were firing on the innocent, people who had been praying. They were firing on the innocent, who were begging for help, for pity, their rosaries in their hands, their little handkerchiefs full of tears, their Bibles in their hands. But you cannot fight bullets with a rosary, a handkerchief, or a Bible. No, and many of them had nothing at all in their hands, they were emptyhanded and facing the guns of Fort Dimanche.

With my own eyes, I saw people fall by the dozens, and then the men of Fort Dimanche who ran out to them grabbed them by the feet and pulled them into the prison, like garbage. I begged the people not to throw rocks—in the state they were in, so frightened, so angry, trying to defend their brothers, they had gathered up a few rocks and were throwing them, an understandable reaction, but useless in such a situation, where all of the might, all of the force, all of the power—all except love, faith, and life—are against you. It was clear that the plot had been hatched long before, and everything was going the way that the evildoers of Fort Dimanche had planned it.

This was another day when I was supposed to die. The bullets were flying above the jeep, around the jeep, and I remember broadcasting live from this scene of death. Into the microphone I said: This is what I am seeing; that is what I am seeing; this is what is happening. I told all. I told the listeners that I didn't even know if I would finish the sentence I had started, because the way the bullets were flying, they might take me and the microphone at any second. And there was a reason I said this, a special reason. That same week, two days earlier, I had been to Fort Dimanche. I had been inside.

Why? That week, knowing that there would be this procession on April 26, we had organized a symbolic funeral for Fort Dimanche in the slum across from my church. It was a funeral for death, for all symbols of death, for all the places where there is death, crime, murder, torture, assassination. We performed the funeral in the name of our Christian faith, the faith we all share across miles and miles of water, brothers and sisters. It was a proper funeral, except that the evildoers from Fort Dimanche descended upon that funeral, and they arrested many people. Passersby, people who were just sitting by the canal, people who were walking past Fort Dimanche—they took them away.

When I heard the news, at about ten in the evening, I went to the police, and they told me the people had been taken to Fort Dimanche. I called Fort Dimanche from the police station, I spoke to the chief there, and he said: Yeah, they're here. I asked him what could be done to free them. He said he didn't think that that could be done so easily. I said: And if I come, will you give them to me? And he said yes. So I said: Okay, I'm on my way.

Maybe it seemed a little naive for me to go running to Fort Dimanche at ten at night to go help out the people arrested by Fort Dimanche because of a symbolic funeral I had said for Fort

Dimanche. Yet there I was, heading for Fort Dimanche, into the belly of the beast. It seems naive, I grant you. But I believe that when your conscience is clean, and your mind is clear, and your faith turns into a motor ready to do what is good and what is correct, well then, at that moment, I believe, it is not you yourself who is really deciding what you will do, but a part of your spirit, in communion with the spirit of good, the spirit of justice, the spirit of liberty—the Holy Spirit. Although it seems that you can choose, in reality you have no choice; the book of your life is already written out for you. Thus, it was not really I who lived, as Saint Paul says, but Jesus Christ who was living through me, as I still wish for him to go on living through me. So at that moment, I felt myself to be completely a missionary, completely a servant to the Spirit, completely in the hands of God, on a mission that went beyond my own weaknesses or strengths, that went beyond what I myself am, and I obeyed, and went to Fort Dimanche, because the Lord commanded me to go.

Well, I got there, in my little white car, and out in front, I ran into a battalion of men from Fort Dimanche, armed to the teeth. They stopped me. "Where are you going?" they shouted at me. "Are you Father Aristide?" I said yes. They said "Hah! It's you. Well, tonight, you'll see, you'll find out." I listened to them, I sat behind the wheel, I left the car running. They continued to shout. "Oh, yes. You'll find out tonight. You're the one who sent them all to get rid of us. You're the one who was saying our funeral Mass. Well, tonight, you're going to find out who's boss. Come in." They were lined up on both sides of the road to the entrance. When I got to the gate, I shut off the car and got out. There were men everywhere, and mud, and great puddles of water. "Go on, go inside," they shouted at me. It was a trap, but I knew I would not be taken in this trap, because the force that I had along with me, neither twenty nor forty little soldiers could stop it from triumphing.

When I finally got inside, I saw the chief, but then they turned out all the lights, to intimidate me. They pointed their guns at me, their machine guns. There were men on all sides. I moved forward among them. And I went up the stairs to the inner terrace. Men to my left, men to my right. And then, from among them, a smile on his lips, calm, serene, his two hands in his pockets, without arrogance, the chief appeared. The whole atmosphere changed, because the chief had arrived with his hypocritically courteous attitude, his head down like a beast that submits to the yoke, almost as if he were about to kiss my feet, he was so nice. Diplomacy, however, cannot be confused with true kindness.

But I was on a mission, and I had to obey certain laws of the house. So I obeyed them, for the good of the cause. I gave this man my hand; he invited me to sit down with him, and I sat down with this man. We spoke in French. He began to compliment me. He said that back in 1977, 1978, he had noticed my good work. "It's true," he said, and he had noticed that I was a deep fellow, "it's true," he said, and this and that, and that he had always followed me from afar, that he admired me and that he had asked himself many times when the day would come when he would meet with me, "and, *voila*, that day has come."

And so we talked on, in French, a meaningless patter of hypocritical politesse, for more than an hour in the shadowy, yellow light (for such men will not allow the bright light of solidarity within their false sanctuary), when meanwhile, facing the wall across from me, the twenty or so people who had been arrested were forced to stand with their backs to us and listen.

Finally, I asked him the question: And what is happening with the people you arrested? And he said, gesturing, "There they are." He looked at their backs. "Those are the ones who came to get rid of us. And we are here to protect lives and property, so I arrested them. But since you have intervened for them, I will give them to you." To protect lives and property, I thought to myself. This is a mantra for such men, "to protect lives and property." Whose lives, brothers and sisters? Whose property? Such phrases on the lips of such men make me want to set fires in the streets and burn down buildings and erect walls of righteous fire to protect the lives of the people and the property of the people from such men.

But all I said to him was "Okay."

He said: "Give me a list of their names."

I said, "Okay." I went up to the wall, where my brothers and sisters were suffering in silence, and I asked them their names, and wrote down whatever names they gave. They spoke softly, sometimes I had to ask them several times. Many had tears running down their cheeks. They had been hurt, and they were deathly frightened. They leaned against the wall as if already expecting and submitting to another beating. One man I came to on that line against the wall, his ear was running with blood. He showed no other sign of pain, or of fear, but yet his ear was running with blood. I asked him, "Brother, why does your ear run with blood?" He did not respond. I asked, "Brother, did they beat you?" He hesitated, and then said, "No." I did not insist, for I knew that he was lying in order to save his skin, and that was my goal also.

So I got the chief his list of names as quickly as possible (a humiliating assignment, meant to menace those who had already suffered, and to implicate me in any further suffering they might undergo), and I took those people out of that dark place of evildoers, the chief accompanying us to the very threshold. He shook my hand there, and of course I thanked him very nicely. The minute we got far enough away, my people opened up, crying, sobbing, telling of their suffering in that place, because once they felt they had escaped from the hand of death, they were ready to tell the story of all that had befallen them in that short time.

Thus, brothers and sisters, you can see why I felt so close to death two days later as the shots rang out in front of Fort Dimanche. I knew what beast lived within that hideous fortress, I knew the pain he liked to inflict. Fort Dimanche itself is just a building, but men—men with the spirits of beasts—have turned it into a killing ground, a concentration camp. Haiti is just a third of a small Caribbean island, but men—men with the spirits of beasts—have turned it into a killing ground, a concentration camp.

Haiti is a prison. In that prison, there are rules you must abide by, or suffer the pain of death. One rule is: Never ask for more than what the prison warden considers your share. Never ask for more than a cupful of rice and a drink of dirty water each day, or each week. Another rule is: Remain in your cell. Though it is crowded and stinking and full of human refuse, remain there, and do not complain. That is your lot. Another rule is: Do not organize. Do not speak to your fellow prisoners about your plight. Every time you get two cups of rice, another prisoner will go hungry. Every time another prisoner gets two drinks of dirty water, you will go thirsty. Hate your fellow man.

Another rule is: accept your punishment silently. Do not cry out. You are guilty. The warden has decreed it. Live in silence until you die. Never try to escape, for escape means a certain return to this prison, and worse cruelty, worse torture. If you dare to escape in your little boat, the corrections officers from the cold country to the north will capture you and send you back to eke out your days within the confines of your eternal prison, which is Haiti. Fort Dimanche is Haiti. Fort Dimanche is Latin America today. Latin America and Haiti today are Fort Dimanche. Fort Dimanche spits out bullets and tear gas and death. It spews rules, regulations, law, order, decree and death. It vomits on us a system of cruelty, repression, exploitation, misery, and death. If we live by its rules, we will certainly perish beneath its whip.

I say: Disobey the rules. Ask for more. Leave your wretchedness behind. Organize with your brothers and sisters. Never accept the hand of fate. Keep hope alive. Refuse the squalor of the parishes of the poor. Escape the charnel house, and move toward life. Fill the parishes of the poor with hope and meaning and life. March out of the prison, down the hard and pitiless road toward life, and you will find the parishes of the poor gleaming and sparkling with joy in the sunrise at the road's end. Children with strong bodies will run with platefuls of rice and beans to greet their starving saviors. That is your reward. Along that hard and pitiless road toward life, death comes as an honor. But life in the charnel house is a disgrace, an affront to humankind.

The youth of Haiti, as elsewhere in the southern part of our hemisphere, is alive with hope, the hope that escape is possible, the hope that someday we will be able to erect a decent poor man's house on the ruins of the charnel house in which we all now live. That undying hope has expressed itself over and over in the actions of the youth of my country, but never as clearly as in the summer of 1987. That summer was a season that whispered with promise, although it crackled also with the terrible reports of the thunder of repression.

In the north of my country that summer, in July, at a place called Jean-Rabel, a massacre took place. Peasants marching to protest their condition and to demand an end to their exploitation by the ruling class of their region were cut down and slaughtered by the military and the agents of the large landholders there. Hundreds were killed; peasants' houses were looted and burned; the peasant movement was momentarily crushed.

Meanwhile, back in Port-au-Prince, my religious order had decided to move me out of the capital and into a parish filled with people who call themselves my enemies, former members of the Tontons Macoute, generals, the wealthy (the enemies of the Haitian people, in short). I obeyed. Not happily, for I had no wish to leave my people alone to face the repression that was coming. I obeyed because I had vowed to obey, and because to disobey might have brought down an even crueler fate upon my parishioners. So I moved to my new parish. (Such displacements and new assignments are not surprising to you, I am sure, brothers and sisters. . . .)

The youth were worried. A massacre of a movement in the north, and now the displacement of one of their most visible colleagues. They sensed the wave of repression beginning to build against them, and took action to deflect it. Thus, they entered the great cathedral of Port-au-Prince, in all humility, and began a hunger strike before its altar. They called on my religious order and the Haitian bishops to rescind the directive moving me out of the capital, and they called on them to speak out against the massacre that had taken place in Jean-Rabel. After all, it was one of the bishops who, just before the massacre, had said that the peasants of the movement in Jean-Rabel were troublemakers. The Haitian proverb says: "He who says

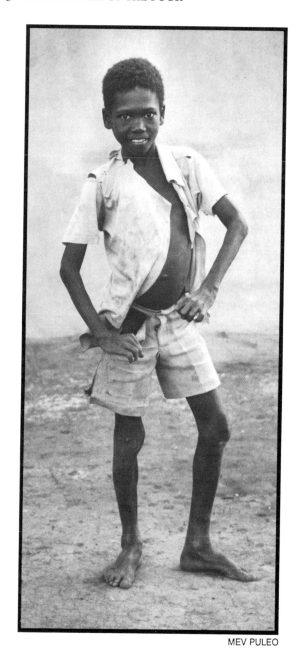

MEV PULEO

'There is the serpent,' has killed the serpent."

After many days of starvation, the hunger strike was successful. It ended in a huge burst of joy within the cathedral as first the bishops and then I came to talk to the thousands who had gathered to support the strikers. I was returned to my parish, the bishops spoke out against what had happened at Jean-Rabel. But that was not the end of the story, my story. As I have said, there is always a first time, but never a last. While the hunger strike continued, it was always in the news. Perhaps there were men who were annoyed at hearing my name repeated. Perhaps there were men who did not like to see the youth take matters into their own hands, however peaceably. Those men, perhaps, got sick of seeing my face on the television and in the newspapers. They never wanted to see my face or my people's faces again. They did not revel in the support we were receiving from Haitians in all walks of life. They sensed a strengthening in the camp of the people, in the parishes of the poor. Our faces were a reproach to those men. All of their hate was concentrated on us, and on me in particular, since I was a symbol of the people I defend, and one man alone is an easier target to mark than all the Haitian people together.

A short time after the young people had their victory at the cathedral, I was to speak at a commemoration honoring the fallen peasants of Jean-Rabel. I had been invited to the celebration at Pont-Sondé two months earlier, and although my safety was in grave doubt after the hunger strike, I did not feel I could now refuse to attend. If the youth had taken a stand on my behalf and on the peasants' behalf at the cathedral in spite of great risks, I felt it was now my turn to take a stand for the youth and for the peasantry, in spite of great risks. I could never forgive myself if I turned my back on history and ran away.

I said a Mass that morning; it was a Sunday in August. It was the first Mass I had said at St. Jean Bosco since my religious order had attempted to move me out. I was surrounded by all the people I had known and loved for so long. I was at home. I did not realize it until much later, but during that Mass, the force of life made me say many things that predicted the death that would rain down on us later the same day. I said that I felt as if I were singing my own funeral Mass, and I did feel that, but I don't know why. That is, I know why now, but I did not know why then. Life and understanding were vibrating in my being, but I was not yet able to interpret their message.

We went to Pont-Sondé. It was a bright, clear day, and the singing and celebration and speeches were to take place inside an old, open-air macaroni factory near the road. My hosts were the Holy Ghost fathers of the area, old friends and colleagues. The parishioners of the region were acting out a series of scenes in commemoration of the massacre at Jean-Rabel, and I felt a spirit of profound communion, of extraordinary, evangelical solidarity with them. It had already been a day of deep emotion for me, a day of return. For almost a month, I had been away from my own parish, but that morning, I had returned to the altar to say Mass. Now, at Pont-Sondé, once again, I felt myself in the midst of my people.

I had been reunited with them that day, and I felt an almost physical bond with my fellow Christians there. I felt renewed by their belief, and inspired by their understanding of Haiti. I felt proud to be invited by my Holy Ghost friends. I felt honored to be speaking along with Father Jean-Marie Vincent, who had worked with the peasants of Jean-Rabel, and who also was risking much by coming before the people in this unprotected way. I felt strong, strengthened by the parishioners' faith. I felt that they were leading me by the hand to new heights, to greater courage, to high places from which I would have a better view and gain a better understanding of the whole Haitian tableau, where I would be better able to receive the messages that I felt were being sent to me and to them by the force of life, which is God.

So when Father Max Dominique signaled me to come before the crowd after Jean-Marie had preached, I was not afraid. I was standing next to Father Max when I heard a sound like a gun being fired. And of course, it *was* a gun being fired. They fired over and over, several men. As they fired, we realized it was real, not a game. Father Max tried to calm the crowd, but people were falling and running in all directions. Near me, I could see three men in hats, wearing white, revolvers in hand, shooting in different directions.

One of them pointed his gun directly at me, standing there. I was standing there because at that moment I was unable to run and leave everybody. I could not take to my heels like a bad pastor, and leave my sheep behind to face the guns. Even though it was obvious that, strategically speaking, it would have been better for me to protect myself, I was incapable of it. I felt calm, and I stood there, and I saw the gun pointed at me and I saw the smoke coming from the gun and I heard the noise of the bullets. He missed me, and began again, and again I saw the smoke and heard the noise, and he missed me again. And then I saw him begin to move backward, and surely his hand must have trembled, because he shot again, and again he missed. And then suddenly I heard a woman say: "Lie down!" and she grabbed my foot, and I found myself beneath a mountain of people who were protecting me, and then they led me out of the place, and they put me into a yellow jeep with two French development workers in it and a bunch of children, and they made me lie down on the floor of the jeep, and drove off. And the children were crying and saying, Is that Father Aristide?, because all around the place, everyone was saying that the men with guns were looking for me. Poor children.

They drove me to the house of the Holy Ghost Fathers; I arrived with one shoe on, because I had lost the other in the panic. I asked the French development workers to return to the scene and find the Holy Ghost Fathers and my other friends, and let them know I was alive and safe, so that they would not continue to expose themselves to death on my behalf. When the fathers and my other friends returned to the residence, they brought with them my shoe; even at the time, it amazed me to see that shoe. Such an unnecessary kindness done for me, in the midst of chaos. It made me want to laugh or cry about the inappropriateness of human feeling, that anyone would think of my silly shoe at a moment like this, with gunfire all around. And of course it was one of the youths who had been in the hunger strike who found my shoe for me. Unending goodness in unimportant matters as well as the gravest issues. I was inordinately grateful for that shoe because it was returned to me with such love. I have always saved that shoe. To me, it is precious.

Then we sat down to talk: Should we go back to Port-au-Prince that evening, or should we not go back? Should we stay at the Holy Ghost Fathers' house, or should we not stay? All of our options were full of risk. In the end, we decided to go back to Port-au-Prince. It was about six o'clock. Rain was falling, and night would soon come. We left in a convoy of several cars; the one in which I rode was the last.

We arrived at the small Army post near Freycineau. The rain was falling. Night was all around us. They were searching our cars. They took down our license plate numbers. They had already taken down all the numbers of the cars that had been at the commemoration at Pont-Sondé, and they were checking them against our numbers. But the first car had not been at the commemoration, so they didn't pay too much attention to them. When they got to the car I was riding in, they looked inside, they checked our license. There were many of them, carrying sticks, machetes and revolvers. They were nearly naked, just wearing shorts or underwear, and some were completely naked. They were coming and going, from the Army post to the car and back.

While they were searching us, the other cars went forward, about a hundred meters, where they came up short against a huge barricade that blocked the highway. My friends started to negotiate with the men at the barricade to see if they would allow them to pass through. Meanwhile, the men mistook Axel Martial—a young, bearded seminarian of the Holy Ghost order who was traveling with our convoy—for me, and they made him get out of his car. A group of the bandits descended on him and began to beat him, when one among them cried out, "No! Father Aristide does not have a beard," and they let Axel go. So they got ready for the moment when I would arrive at the barricade, and they would do to me what they had been going to do to Axel. But of course where we were (I was with Father Jean-Marie, Fathers Antoine Adrien and William Smarth, and a Canadian seminarian), we had no idea what was happening up at the barricade. We watched the men going back and forth from the post to the car, and we of course realized something was up, but we didn't know what, even though we could see with our own eyes that we were dealing with criminals, evildoers, assassins, men capable of anything.

But the force of life was still with us, even in the midst of their deadly plotting, even as they forced us from our car, and searched every crevice of it, and made us stand in the dark and the rain, and the big chief with his big gun came toward us in the night, and the whole time, you never knew when a bullet was going to hit you in the head, when a kick or a knife thrust or a smack from a stick or a hit from the butt of a revolver was going to fall upon you, when they were going to receive the order to drag you into the underbrush, or if instead they would get an order to let your car go through with those they no longer wanted, while keeping with them those they were hunting for. You just stood there waiting for whatever was going to happen. Once they were finished searching the car in front of us, they made them leave.

When they finished searching our car, they said, get in, and it seemed a little odd, but you take a deep breath because it's over. And then the criminals let us go, knowing we would soon arrive back in their midst at the barricade. And there they were, more of them, with rifles, revolvers, sticks and rocks in the middle of the rainstorm. Some wore red T-shirts, some wore shorts, a few wore hats, but others didn't; they were not wearing hoods over their heads because they didn't mind showing their faces while they did their dirty work. And then, the first rock was thrown into one of our headlights, and smashed it. Another, and the second headlight went out. A third, and the windshield was shattered. We said, this is worse, this is more serious. Ah! But we were still calm, because what could they do worse than kill us? We prayed. Jean-Marie in the front seat took the worst of the rocks. (He still has the mark of one on his temple. He will always carry that mark.)

All around us, the men were shouting. Their commentaries showered down around us like raindrops. "Where are the communists? Where is Father Aristide? Give us the communists. You're talking too much, let's act! Let's get our hands on him!

Let's get this over with!" They were talking about death, about killing. They talked like this while they were waiting to receive the order to execute us. Meanwhile, the rocks kept flying. And Father Adrien tried to reason with the men. "Pont-Sondé is where we are coming from," he told them. "This was what we were doing. Nothing odd, nothing bad." But they didn't listen to reason, and one told Father Smarth to get out.

"You all are talking too much! Get out," he said. The man had his machete in his hand and he was holding it in the air, and as clearly as I imagined the next moment then, I can see it now: I could see Father Smarth's head in the hands of that man after he finished cutting through his neck with his bloody machete, and I thought to myself, the first one down will be Father Smarth. They opened the door of the car and Father Smarth got out, and the man's machete was in the air over Father Smarth's head. And then the force of life overcame the man, and he let his machete fall, and he shoved Father Smarth against the car, and Father Smarth fell, and a machete shattered through the back window and the evildoers were attacking on all sides, and I was bleeding—I still do not know how I was injured.

Then I heard one of them say: "Father Aristide is in this car. Let's go get some gas and pour it over them. You all talk too much, these are communists, let's burn them." They beat at Father Adrien's door to make him get out, but he just kept talking to them, and while he was talking they threw rocks at him. He tried to protect his face with his hands, and the rocks smashed into his wrists. Rocks were falling all over us, we had no protection against them, all the windows were already shattered. The rocks were falling; gas—and then fire—would come soon. We kept thinking of the courageous martyr nuns of Salvador. We thought of the moments before the deaths of all martyrs. Death was very near, death was wearing shorts and slamming a machete through glass, death was walking and running and shouting all around us. Death was bringing the fire of the martyrs to snuff out life.

But the force of life did not retreat before death, and it burst forth in the voice of Jean-Marie who shouted at the Canadian seminarian: Go left! Go left! because Jean-Marie had seen a little hole open up on the left of the barricade, like a little window of life through which light was shining. Imagine it, we were in the dark, in the rain, with our headlights blown out, sticks, rocks, and guns surrounded us; the criminals were standing there with their claws out, the fire was coming, and there was Jean-Marie, shouting to go left. The driver didn't understand. He could do nothing. So we shouted: Go left! Go! but this time in English, because we realized finally that the driver didn't speak much French and couldn't understand any French in his panic, and our shout in English burst into his head like a shout of life and suddenly he stepped on the gas and turned sharply left, and he slammed the car through that barricade, and we were away from death, for the moment.

Still, what can you do on a highway in the rain, in the dark, in a car with no lights? Where can you go to escape from the evildoers? But our strength, which was the strength of life, of God, a strength that never turns to weakness, defeated the evildoers, because somehow, they were not able to run and catch up with us, even though our car could do nothing but roll slowly along in the dark, swerving from side to side because we had no lights and the rain was pouring in on us through our broken windows, and we could not see at all where we were going. Rain was pouring in on us, the night was pitch black, and the road kept escaping out from under our tires, but the force of life pushed that car far enough and fast enough to flee the ferocity of death.

We did not know what to do. Was it better to keep going blind or to leave the car somewhere and run into the hills?

But God told us to keep on going, and we went forward in our wounded car in spite of everything, hoping we would get to a church nearby or be able to stop at the retreat of a Protestant group we recalled in the area. And we drove into the Protestants' place, and we were happy to receive a welcome that went beyond all religious differences, that went to the heart of our shared belief in the same Lord, the same Christian faith. Yes, they welcomed us, and without giving too many details, we explained that there had been an accident and people were wounded, and they gave us shelter and first aid. There we spent the night, uncertain whether we would live to see the sun rise, because we were still not very far from Freycineau, and the evildoers could have come at any moment and taken us away. We were waiting for life to continue or for death to reappear, we did not know which.

So we stayed with the Protestants that night, because the priests at the nearby church did not have a car that was in good enough shape to come get us (always the same stories of old cars, broken-down cars, cars with no gas, flat tires, the story of my poor country), and the Protestants did not want to drive us in the night in our wounded car over to the nearby church. They felt it was too dangerous, and I believe they were right.

When morning light began to come, at about five in the morning the next day, they went with us and our same driver got behind the wheel of our same car with all its windows broken but the motor still working, and we went to the church in nearby Montrouis. People had already heard the news, had heard that we were dead, that we had disappeared, that we were in hiding or in prison, they had heard about the rocks and the car and the barricade, and they were gathering to see if they could find the car, and to look at it, and see if what they had heard was true. The friends who had been with us in their cars at the barricade and who had escaped before us or after us knew that something terrible had happened, but they did not know if we were dead or alive. No one in the country, no one in the world knew if we were dead or alive.

When we finally managed to get the news out to some of our friends and to our family — by our family, I don't mean our mothers and fathers, but our true family, the family of God, the people of Haiti — a convoy of friends came up from Port-au-Prince to provide us with security so that we could return to the capital and receive treatment for our wounds, especially Father Adrien and Jean-Marie. And many friends came, close friends, and therefore we felt safe again for the first time. An ambulance came. And Bishop Constant from Gonaïves came, too: he made an appearance, as did the Papal Nuncio.

We went to the hospital in Port-au-Prince and stayed there

MEV PULEO

two or three days and then moved out to one place and another and another, in order to be safe, because the claws of the evil-doers were still exposed and they were still waiting to get hold of us. And when the four Haitian priests who had been attacked at Freycineau asked the Haitian bishops to say a Mass of grace and thanksgiving with us, they refused. They refused!

Father Smarth, Father Adrien, Father Jean-Marie and I did say that Mass of grace. We said it alone, together, without the bishops. Thousands came to see us alive before them. Thousands of people from all over the capital, politicians and paupers alike, came to hear our voices and to be inspired by the force of life — our lives and their lives — that had emerged breathing and walking, its heart beating strong, from out of the maw of death. Through us, the people gained strength. Through the story of our triumph over the forces of evil, the people were heartened. If we could face death and not die, then they could face death and not die.

Even if we had died at that barricade, we would have lived on in the memories of the people, because our spirit is their spirit. What moves them, moves us also. We speak the words that the spirit of the poor breathes into us. That is our humble role, a simple role, one that requires no learning, no pride, no soutane, no miter. It requires faith only, and of faith we have plenty. It requires a willingness to serve the people, and no machete, no fusillade of rocks, no bullets or rifles or Uzis, no tear gas or bombs, will ever dissuade us from that willingness, from that faith. We are unshakable. Like the poor, we will always be with you. Kill one among us, and we rise up again, a thousand strong.

Brothers and sisters, do I strain your credulity? Is it hard to believe that so many attacks could occur, so many be targeted against the base of the Church? No, I do not think you are surprised by my tale. I do not think so. Surely each and every last one of you has seen the claws of the evildoers come scratching down across the face of a colleague. Surely each and every one of you has known fear as you go about bringing your faith to your congregation, as you speak out about their plight, as you help the poor of your parish to organize. Yes, we are all part of the same battalion, the troops of the Lord, and here in Haiti, we consider every attack against you an attack against us, just as every injury or death that we suffer in our dark corner of the world is a death or injury that you feel, too. Our common struggle reaches across political borders, across mountain ranges, across vast bodies of water. Across the wide spaces of our hemisphere, we hold one another's hands in a long and unbreakable chain of solidarity. Hold on. Don't let go. If you hold my hand, then surely I will not fall. If I support you, surely you will find the strength to go on. We are one.

More than a year went by before the next onslaught. Many things happened during that unmerciful year. We had presidential elections. Twice. Haiti had to prove it was "moving toward democracy." Only if we elected a government would the cold country to our north, and its allies—other former colonizers—send us more money and food. Of course, that money and that food corrupt our society: The money helps to maintain an armed force against the people; the food helps to ruin our national economy; and both money and food keep Haiti in a situation of dependence on the former colonizers. The first "show" presidential elections were attacked by the armed forces—as well as agents of the ruling economic class and the old regime—because the men with guns feared, whether rightly or wrongly, that the president who would be elected would not continue to support them. Two presidential candidates were assassinated. Scores of voters were massacred.

The second presidential elections were calm. The puppet of the armed forces was selected president in the farcical process, and remained president for more than four months, until the general who had taken over after Duvalier fell got tired of the new president's civilian ways, and deposed him. Now when that general came back to power, he was even more brutal, more vicious, crueler than he had been before, and times got worse for the people and for those who worked with the people. Everyone was frightened, and many, many opposition leaders and human-rights activists and men and women like us — those who worked inside the people's church — were in hiding, or half in hiding.

Death squads were in the streets every night. Every night there was gunfire. Every morning there were bodies. In the streets, they rounded up the orphans who came to me for shelter and food and affection, and took them to Fort Dimanche and beat them till they had marks across their bodies. They hunted down literacy workers, and killed them. They followed journalists through the streets and threatened them over the telephone. They tortured and killed members of youth movements. They tortured and killed members of peasant movements. Students were slain. A priest was kicked out of the country. The Haitian bishops remained silent.

During this time of nightmare, when the light of life and the light of solidarity burned at their lowest intensity, we tried to keep hope alive in the hearts of the people. We burrowed deep into our shadowy dens, lit only by that faint but promising light, looking for the food of life, which is hope. We found hope there, in the very depths of our being, and we brought it up in our bare hands to share with our brothers and sisters. We dug beneath the dying roots of the corrupt system, foraging for the embers of life, and we found them.

For hope is always there, even in the darkest times, even in the most obscure places, as long as you and I have the energy and the commitment to search for it, and then to bring it forward, to share it. Hope is there, no matter how heavily the boots of the Army tread upon it, in their effort to stamp it out. Hope is there like a smoldering fire that cannot be extinguished. The fire is there beneath the earth — like the fire of a charcoal pit — and all it takes is a little air, a little oxygen, a bit of fanning to make it ignite and explode and burst through the surface like a refiner's fire, a purging blast of heat that will someday — if we work hard and carefully enough together — turn into a steady, even flame over which we can cook good, nourishing food for all the people; someday, that purifying furnace will heat a decent, poor man's kitchen stove.

That is our work, to fan the fire of hope and turn it into a tool for the people. We tried to do that in those dark days, to help the people think in useful ways about their future, and about the continuing possibility of burning their way out of their hellish prison. It was not an easy task, and each time one of us spoke out, we were marked even more clearly for violent death. We, and those who surrounded us. Our friends. Our family. The Haitian people.

Let me go on with my story. More than a year after the ambush at Freycineau, another man with another gun came into my church on another Sunday morning while I was celebrating Mass, and he was disarmed by the congregation. I took the gun and the bullets, and tried to give them to the Nuncio, as I had done after the last such incident. But times had changed, and I was no longer beloved by the Nuncio. In the old days, he was proud of me; I was part of the movement to rid the country of Duvalier, and so was he. But his interest in change stopped with the person of the dictator; he was not troubled by the continuation of the unjust, corrupt system that the dictator had managed. Instead, he was angered by my continued outcry against the continued injustice.

No, the Nuncio had no use for me anymore, and even the slender ties that supposedly bind one member of our Church to the other would not force him to do me the service of taking that gun off my hands, which it was his bounden duty to do. I called therefore a justice of the peace, and two came, and I surrendered the gun to them.

Two days later, as usual, I celebrated a youth Mass. Every Tuesday evening at St. Jean Bosco we had that Mass. On this particular Tuesday, however, I did not want to say the Mass. I told the youth: There is too much tension. It is too dangerous. We must not celebrate this Mass. But they insisted. They said: We come here for this, for you to celebrate Mass, for us to demonstrate our faith. And so the Mass was said. I said a quick Mass, so that they would be able to go home before night fell. But before they could leave the church, a hail of rocks began to fall upon us, upon the church and the courtyard. Men had surrounded the place, and the rocks fell. The rocks rained down upon us, and shots rang out. We hid and waited until they went away. This time, they went away. But that night was only a warning, a small taste of the horror that was to come, and soon.

That whole week in September 1988, rumors were flying around town. Sunday, the Tontons Macoute would come to attack us. That was the rumor. For days, all I heard about was what was going to take place at St. Jean Bosco. Of course, it was not the first time I had heard such rumors. They were always saying that the Macoutes would come to stamp us out, to kill us, to ransack the church. If I had listened to each and every rumor, we would not have said Mass more than ten times during the three years after Duvalier fell. Threats, attacks, rumors, news of death, reports of assassination attempts, reports of men who were receiving money to kill me — that's what I was hearing. It was the same as usual, but more intense. So I listened, I heard, I continued to listen, I continued to hear, because I generally like to make decisions that correspond to the opinions of the majority of the people I work with.

Although they were frightened, the youths from my church decided on Saturday that we would have Mass on Sunday as usual. But when I heard (from someone at City Hall, where the massacre was being planned) that men wearing red armbands would attack us the next morning, I called another meeting of the youths, to give them this new information. I didn't want to decide alone. That night, Saturday night, we decided that the six o'clock Mass would be said as usual on Sunday morning (because I did not usually say the early morning Mass, and thus that Mass might not attract the anger of the men with red armbands), and then depending on how many people came for six o'clock Mass and what the atmosphere was like, we would decide whether or not to say the nine o'clock Mass where I ordinarily preached.

The night passed. Many of the young people stood watch. During the six o'clock Mass, I remained in my bedroom in a building across the courtyard from the church. The youths came to tell me that there had been very few congregants at the Mass. I said, all right, let's close the church and there will be no Mass at nine. I went back upstairs.

At eight-thirty, the telephone rang in my room. I picked it up, and it was a youth downstairs in the office near the church, who told me that many people had arrived at the church to hear Mass, and that there must be a nine o'clock Mass. I said: "Listen: I thought we had already decided that there would be no nine o'clock Mass this morning."

And the person on the other end of the phone said: "It is not my decision that I am telling you of, it is the decision of the Lord's people, who have come to Mass and who expect to hear Mass sung."

I was hesitant. I wanted to know whether they understood the risk, did they know how dangerous it was. And this person said, yes, they know the dangers, but they know also that their faith tells them that they must not run when the enemy approaches; they must not let the enemy chase them away from the Mass. They are not coming to battle, they have no argument with any man, they have come simply to pray, why should they not be allowed to gather for prayer? "We must have the Mass," the youth said.

It was a hard moment for me, personally. I knew that people were receiving large amounts of money to assassinate me that very morning, so personally, I was not inclined to go and stand before a crowd. And indeed, I told myself, if I went, would not my presence bring down on the heads of my congregation the rage of the assassins? Better that they find me and kill me when I am by myself, I thought. But at the same time, I had a nagging fear in the back of my mind. The assassins would not know until they got to the church that I was not there. When they failed to get their hands on me, would they not mindlessly attack my congregation out of frustrated rage? The decision was not an easy one for me to make, because I was so anxious to perceive all of the possible consequences of each of the possible options, both for me and for my congregation. And then I thought to myself, well, now, what if the assassins come, and I'm not there, and they do attack my people anyway? Won't many say that I knew the assassins were coming, and I fled, abandoning my people? And, indeed, would that not be the case? Out of fear for myself, perhaps, I was making the excuse that my presence might hurt my people, when actually, they might suffer whether or not I was among them. And that was what made me decide to present myself for the Mass. I thought to myself, every other time, I have been there to suffer with my people; this time, perhaps the worst time, I must be there also.

So I said: I will come to the place called Calvary. If this was to be my last day, as it seemed, then I would carry my cross, and the struggle for light and life would continue because God is life. So I got dressed up in my room, and came downstairs and two friends came to meet me, a girl and a boy. They accompanied me, and in their voices, in their faces, in every inch of them, I could feel fear, a shiver of tension. And I said to them: This is our Calvary, like Jesus who ascended the Cross.

It was not an easy decision, and as I said this to them, I could feel rise in me like a current of suffering the courage that was holding us together, and I could smell the smell of death upon us. I could feel death coming for us. I had felt death come for me before, but not for others. This time was different, and I could feel it, could smell it. This time, I knew that my presence might put my people in danger. That burden felt like a heavy cross, a cross of human suffering, upon my back. But I knew also that my absence might put more of them in worse danger, and so I came—because I had to come—to the place that is called Calvary. When your fate has been decided, you have no choice. What seems like choice is not choice; it is the hand of Providence writing out the book of your life for you. And so I went into the church, and up to the blessed altar.

The reading for the day was from St. Matthew. Jesus was talking to his partisans: "If any man will come after me, let him deny himself, and take up his cross, and follow me." The chapter continues: "For whosoever will save his life shall lose it: and whosoever will lose his life for my sake shall find it." The words comforted me. They calmed me. They quieted my fears.

That Sunday, many people had decided to show their respect for the Constitution by wearing white (the color that was worn in March 1987, when the Constitution was approved by a popular vote), and some of my people were wearing white, it is true. But the rest of my people were dressed as they dressed every Sunday to come to my church: in the colors of love, in the colors of faith, in the rainbow colors of courage, in patriotic raiment. The fact that they were there at all, at St. Jean Bosco, on a day that everyone knew would be full of rage, was testimony to their patriotism and courage. They were not there naively, unknowing. They were there to show that they had taken up the cross of Jesus, and that they would carry that cross through a lifetime of menaces and threats. That Sunday, I told them that they did not really need to ask the Lord for his forgiveness for their sins, because the courage that had brought them to this particular church on this particular day had purified them utterly. My people were clothed in robes of crimson and of purple, waiting to be scourged and mocked, and crucified.

And so I said to the congregation: "Let us begin."

And we had just finished reading the Gospel — not more than five minutes had passed — offertory, consecration — when I heard the first cry go up from the street, the first smashing of rocks, a few first shots fired. A wind of panic rose up in the street and was blowing toward us in the church, blowing along the backs of the men who were shouting and throwing rocks, shooting guns. While I was trying to calm the congregation and stop them from hurting one another in the panic, bullets began crisscrossing the church in front of me. One round passed just in front of me and lodged itself in the tabernacle. They missed me and hit the tabernacle. With the microphone in my hand, I was thinking that a pastor must stay and die before, or in the place of, his sheep, and not run and leave them behind. I was wondering how to stop the panic from overwhelming the congregation. And I was wondering whether the power of our solidarity would make our force equal to theirs, whether we would be able to oppose

MAGGIE STEBER

them with a prophetic, evangelical resistance, and stop the panic that was about to disperse us, that was about to let them kill us more quickly, one by one. I shouted to my congregation: "Blessed be the Eternal! Blessed be the Eternal!" And the bullets kept smashing through the church.

People say that ten or twenty people died that day at St. Jean Bosco. The official version is ten to twenty. The exact number depends on your source. But it is the same as the massacre in front of Fort Dimanche: no one will ever be able to say with any certainty how many died that day at St. Jean Bosco. I myself could see them dragging bodies of parishioners out in front of the church in order to load them into cars, while the bullets were still flying through the chancel and the nave, and up and down the aisles, over the heads of my people, and piercing their flesh. The men with red armbands did not always drag the wounded and dead all the way out because there was so much confusion, and many of the injured and dead were left in the church, heaped in a pile, to die later by fire and be among the uncounted martyrs.

Everyone was running, trying to find a place to hide. One man was shot in the outside courtyard, and collapsed and died in the inner courtyard, with his Bible in his hand. Bullets were zinging left and right. I saw a pregnant woman screaming for help in the pews, and holding onto her stomach. A man had just speared her there, and she was bathed in red blood. Another priest was trying to organize people to give the woman first aid. I saw an American journalist running up and down the aisle with torn clothes; the men with red armbands had torn the clothing, trying to hurt the journalist. A group of young women were in the front courtyard and were attempting to resist the onslaught, attempting to resist, with our own kind of arms, the heavy weapons that the men were using against us from the street—this was a prophetic, historic resistance that we will never forget.

Our weapon was our solidarity, as we stood together, unified, and our weapons were rocks, that we used to stop the men from coming over the top of the courtyard wall and getting into the church to murder us all. If we had not resisted in this fashion, what happened to us at St. Jean Bosco would have been a hundred times worse than the election day massacre in November 1987. Hundreds and hundreds of us would have died beneath the stick, or of punches and kicks, or speared at the end of a steel pike, or shot through the head, or cut into pieces with machetes and knives and daggers—the murderers were ready to do anything and everything, and the Haitian Army had surrounded the murderers in silence, their guns at their sides, watching as the assassins went about their business.

This was a great moment that showed pacifists against the bloody-minded, the people of God against assassins. The criminals—Tonton-Macoute Duvalierist thugs, paid with a few dollars and a bottle of rum, and prepared for any act—were looking to spit death into the faces of those who were fighting for life with no weapons of death in their hands. During this whole time, as death rained down on us, across from the church stood the Haitian Army, back behind the church stood Fort Dimanche, and, of course, neither one attempted to stop the killings. They watched. God have mercy on those who watch evil and do nothing. They are as guilty as the murderer. Often, they are his accomplice.

Yes, this lasted three hours, and meanwhile, what did the Church do, what help did it give us?

My Salesian superior heard about what was happening, he gathered up his courage, he crossed through the battle zone and came to the courtyard of St. Jean Bosco. A valiant man. He came into the midst of the battle and fought to save us, negotiated with the leaders of the criminals, allowed the assassins to humiliate him, offered them drinks, did everything to calm the situation, and bravely worked alongside us to end the killing.

At this same moment, where was the Nuncio? What was he doing? He was not there. He came late. When he finally descended from his house, he did not come all the way. He remained aloof. Across the street from the burning church, watching and waiting, I am not sure for what.

And then there was a Salesian sister, who is not afraid of anyone. And she came through the battlefield to help us, too. She braved all the dangers. But she was there only to save the

Salesians, and was willing and ready to offer up to the wolves those of us who were not in the Salesian family, friends of mine, friends of other priests. She would save the Salesians and throw the rest to the devil. Ah, my sister! All persons are human beings, and to be cherished.

There is a multitude of ways to deal with death, sisters and brothers, is there not? There are valiant youths who go face to face with death, and battle it with their poor rocks; there are men and women, full of courage, who come from the wings onto death's own stage and talk with death, trying to convince death to retreat; there are men and women, cold-blooded, who watch death operate as though the whole thing were a film of great interest, men and women who do nothing but observe the battle scene; and there are men and women who see death coming and save only their own, who do not care for the rest of poor, sweet humanity.

Meanwhile, fire had run its course through the church. The assassins had doused the building with gasoline and set it on fire. The roof of my beautiful, beloved church had fallen in, smoke was pouring out, and all Port-au-Prince could see that hell had burst up in our midsts, as though the end of the world had appeared in the fire's flames. It was odd for most people to watch St. Jean Bosco burn when on all sides, the church was surrounded by police headquarters. But the police crossed their arms, with their guns in hand, and protected the criminals who burned down the church, and who kept on killing and robbing with impunity. Fire in the church, fire in human minds.

The police finally uncrossed their arms and began to act. They opened the gate to the inner courtyard. They beat it with the butts of their guns, along with the men with the red armbands. They opened the gate, which we had locked for our protection. My superior came to see what they were doing, but they paid him no attention. They cut the chain; they opened the gate. They worked together, the police and the criminals. The assassins burst into the inner courtyard and continued their rampage. "So you are the ones who are playing guerilla!" they shouted at the hundred or so cowering congregants who were huddled in the courtyard. They pointed their guns at these innocent people and forced them to put their hands above their heads, as though my congregation were armed, a congregation like mine, made up of market women, and cart haulers, and cobblers and seamstresses and woodworkers and blacksmiths and mothers and fathers with their children. Soon after, the criminals evacuated the courtyard.

Then we were alone. Alone with the police and a bunch of criminals in civilian clothes who were carrying heavy arms. A few Salesian fathers, we were, and a few close friends, one of whom was the well-known leader of a peasant movement in central Haiti. A colonel came and told us we must leave immediately, but that he could not assure our security.

That was the Haitian Army, tried and true, protector of life and property. They had watched us burn, watched us die, watched us speared through the stomach and screaming with pain, and now, they could not assure our security. Such is the power of the Army in our lands, brothers and sisters, such are the protectors of the rotting system, slaughterers of change and progress. Strong and loyal to their masters, vicious and cowardly in their dealings with the people. They rise up out of the bosom of the people, from the heart of the slums, only to turn around and attack the people, their own family. And all for the sake of a job and a few dollars a week. Just as the Army could not guarantee my security and the security of my brothers and sisters in Christ on that fateful Sunday morning, so they cannot either guarantee the safety of Haiti, of the Haitian citizen. It is up to us to guarantee our own security. It is up to us to wrest power from this vile old institution. The men of the Army, men of the people, must make a new choice — to protect their brothers and sisters, and not their masters.

And so we had to go. I packed up my little valise, threw in a few shirts, and headed for the stairs with the Salesian sister I have spoken of before. She was my security, my bodyguard. (And to my mind, she was a better bodyguard than all the Haitian Army.) We were going down the stairs when one of the criminals nodded at me ever so slightly and whispered: "Don't show yourself." I retreated. (The men, I later learned, were prepared to shoot me the minute my face appeared at the door downstairs.) Then suddenly the colonel reversed his order and told us to remain.

They were going to search the residence. Another slap of humiliation: they would search us. The criminal was going to search the innocent. The men with guns were going to search those without arms. Those who had committed the crimes were going to search their victims. Brothers and sisters, we live in an upside-down world. In our hemisphere, the police are the criminals, the saints are the sinners, those who are outlawed are those who wish to live in a state that respects the law. The Army protects our lives by killing us, and then they tell us that they are burning down the church in order to defend it.

(The evildoers have always used the Army against the people, as did the cold country to our north when it occupied Haiti from 1915 to 1934. They set up the Haitian Army, they trained it to work against the people. I say this in order to force Haitian soldiers of my time to face up to this truth; I say this so that in the midst of the Army itself, the men will recognize that they, the sons of the people, are being positioned against themselves, who are the issue of the people's womb. Thus, in the Army itself, the soldiers are victims; they are not evil soldiers arrayed against civilians, but an Army arrayed against a people and against all of the children of the people. The irony is that they themselves are the people, children of the people. Only filthy dollars can corrupt them and make them stand firm against the will of the people, their people.)

I accepted the word of the soldiers that they were to search our residence, and I went back upstairs and sat down on a rocking chair in the common room, with my back to the television. At least fifty men, some of them in uniform, some of them in civilian dress, all of them carrying rifles or machine guns, surrounded me. Into my little room down the hall, almost as many were stuffed, and searching. One of the men with me sat down across from me and pointed his gun at my heart, and he began to yell, to curse, to storm at me, always with his gun pointed at me so that after a while I began to wonder whether he might shoot me just by accident, he was so angry. There was another behind me, watching the angry man, and I think the one behind me was stopping the one in front of me from hurting me. I just sat there looking at the angry fellow, and of course this made him angrier, because he could not understand how a man who was about to die, a man who had seen what had happened to his church, what had happened to his people, what was going to happen to him, could just sit there calmly, waiting. And I was thinking at that moment that he could do anything with me, because anyone who is willing to shower blood down on a church where everyone is in prayer, and to do that before the whole world, without shame, would find it a simple thing to eliminate one man.

Eventually, he did jump up and said: "Search him! It's time to get rid of him." He shouted and yelled like a crazy man, and an argument broke out between him and the man behind me. I tipped back my chair so that the two could fight more easily, and suddenly my chair turned and I saw the man who had been behind me and he saw me. I rocked in my rocking chair and he looked at me and said to the wrathful fellow, "But I am a class-mate of Father Aristide's." And their argument grew more heated, just as a fire grows twice its size when you pour gasoline on it instead of water. One wanted to defend me, the other to kill me. Now their camp was divided, and they were confused. And this division among them came about not because of my powers or my intelligence or my cleverness, or anything I had done, but because of the power of life, which thrust itself forward as it did for St. Paul, to prove that it was life and God, and to confound the evildoers.

Well, the angry one said, "Let's take the guy downstairs, and when everyone is out of here, we'll execute him." But the man behind me was not going to let me go alone with such a man in charge or put me in such irresponsible hands, and so for the time being I was saved. Then the soldiers and armed civilians who were searching my room called on me to go watch the search, and I did as I was told, and it was hard for me, because fifty or so men were in my little room, ripping apart my library, looking for bad books. They found something by Marx, and shouted "Communist," and I believe they would have executed me then and there for that one sin of reading Marx, if it hadn't been for another colonel, who talked them out of it. (It is always important to remember that within a group of men and women, no matter how good or how bad, there are always factions. Factions are what make change possible.)

The search wore on, from the head to the tail of the building, in each priest's room. Every corner was searched. Things were stolen. The title of every book in every room was read, by those among the searchers who knew how to read. This was all part of their strategy. They did not think they would find arms, or grenades, or a blueprint for overthrowing the government, or a box full of funds to finance the revolution, sitting right there in a residence of priests. What they were doing was taking their time, waiting for night to fall, so that in the cover of darkness and anonymity, they could execute me and the peasant leader who was there with us, and no one would ever know the face of the man who had pulled the trigger. It was already five in the afternoon, and the massacre had begun long before, at nine in the morning. They were waiting out the clock, slowly sauntering through the hallways of our home as the sun began to set. Luckily for us, the sun takes a long time to set over Haiti. Even smoke billowing out of a church on a Sunday morning and afternoon cannot obscure the rays of our strong sun.

And finally, finally, the soldiers left, saying their mission had been accomplished, and leaving us alone with the armed civilians, the most ferocious of the hoard. But my friends and colleagues and sisters and brothers gathered around me, and we went down the stairs together, and the criminals did not stop us. We got into a car at the door of the residence, and we drove through the inner courtyard to a gate that opens onto the churchyard, and we drove through the churchyard to another gate that opens onto the street. No route has ever seemed so long to me, though the whole way is not more than a few hundred meters. The men with red armbands were still standing around in each courtyard, in the street. Their hands were full of the counterfeit money that had been paid to them by bigger criminals, their hips were stacked with guns, their heads were full of drugs given to them by bigger criminals, they were ready for more viciousness.

But that which was to be done, was already done; that which was to be said, had been said; those who were to rise up, rose up; those who were to fall, had fallen. What had been stirred up there that day had been stirred up for good, and now, the force of life had come together: it enveloped me; it planned our escape; it opened the way; it opened the gate. It did all that need be done. And the evildoers stood there in the street; they saw us pass and they did not see me pass; they knew I was passing by, but they did not feel me pass by; we went through the midst of them and they were not moved against us. And thence, we went to the place to which we were to go. And we were hidden, by the grace of the Lord.

Hearing tell of all these events, people have wondered how it is that death did not sweep me away that afternoon. But I believe that if you look for the answer to this question with reason only, you will not find it, because the answer lies deeper down and farther away than reason alone can travel. People say it was magic. Well, if you call the work of God magic, then it was magic. Some have said the charms of voodoo—my country's other religion—saved us. Well, if you call God a charm, then surely it was a charm that saved us. What spared us from death that day, who knows, but it demonstrates surely how far a seemingly weak force can go in order to vanquish a greater force. It is not a thing that happens often.

This victory, our victory—for indeed, in the end, ours was the victory, the side of the martyrs triumphed—was achieved for and by the Haitian people in general, and in particular, it was achieved for and by the congregation of St. Jean Bosco, who were supposed to disappear in a hail of bullets and a ball of fire, and who, instead, reemerged from death carrying the embers of hope and life, and who stand today next to the bodies of their dead comrades, in the shadow of our burned-out church, and hold out hope and life to the rest of the Haitian people. We are

MAGGIE STEBER

more blessed when we preach to a hungry congregation from the top of a dusty pile of cinders than when we preach to the well-fed from a luxurious altar inside a magnificent cathedral.

Thus would God have us walk through the valley of death and find ourselves, our voyage at an end, at the sunlit crossroads of life; so would God have us travel nightmarish highways of rain and gloom and murder only to pull into a carefree village at sunrise in our exhausted car with its four flat tires; so would God have us fight for life in battlefields of blood and entrails, and harvest life from fields of bones and ashes. There in the wasteland where you had not thought to find life, you will suddenly find the signs of God's renewal, blooming and flowering and bursting forth from the dry earth with great energy, God's energy. In the driest month, you will find on the branches' tips new shoots of life. Under the rock in the desert will sprout a flower, a delicate bud of the new life.

Remember that young woman I saw that day, bleeding from her womb, clutching herself where they had speared her, sobbing that she would lose the baby that was growing inside her? Here again is a story of life coming where there should be death. This is the story—finally—of the child called Hope. The woman bled and bled as the assassins rampaged through my church; they had knifed her where they knew it would do the most damage. These are men who see a mother and want to damage what is within her. Insanity. Somehow, the woman, bleeding and sobbing, was brought to a hospital.

Everyone in Port-au-Prince had heard the story of the godless attack against the young mother and her unborn child. And the criminals, that night, after the massacre had ended, went to the university hospital, searching the maternity wards. They had heard that the woman had survived, and they wanted to kill her, to show the people that there was no hope in this world. They made the mothers in the maternity ward lift their white nightgowns to see if they were wounded in the stomach. Indecency. But they never found the woman. She had been taken to another hospital far away, and there—miracle, miracle—she was delivered, by caesarean, of a baby girl, a wounded baby girl, but fine, healthy, more or less undamaged. And that child she called

Esperancia, or Hope. Because the baby's birth showed that the murderers, the assassins, the criminals, the police, the Army, the president and all the president's men could not put an end to Hope in Haiti, could not destroy us, could not wreck our infant aspirations with their knives and spears. Hope's birth showed that a new Haiti could emerge from the wounded body of the old, that in spite of the atrocities visited upon Haiti, she could give forth new life, if only her friends would help her, and shelter her, and protect her, and help her with the birth. Hope is the new generation of my country.

Sometimes, when I think of the tribulations and great suffering that the Haitian people have endured, both at home and on the high seas seeking a better life in other lands; sometimes, when I think of my story over the past three years and the story of the Haitian people during that period, I am reminded of St. Paul's description of his travails:

> Thrice I was beaten with rods, once was I stoned, thrice I suffered shipwreck, a night and a day have I been in the deep;
> In journeyings often, in perils of waters, in perils of robbers, in perils by mine own countrymen, in perils by the heathen, in perils in the city, in perils in the wilderness, in perils in the sea, in perils among the false brethren;
> In weariness and painfulness, in watchings often, in hunger and thirst, in fastings often, in cold and nakedness (2 Corinthians 11:25–27).

Physically, personally, and spiritually, I was rescued, on that day of massacre, from the endless litany of suffering. Like St. Paul, who fled King Aretas's garrison in Damascus, I felt that I had eluded the evildoers, "through a window in a basket . . . let down by the wall." By the merest chance and luck, I had escaped their hands. But we will not always be so lucky, brothers and sisters. The force of life will not always prevail in the short run.

It took the Church in Haiti a long time, a very long time, to respond to what had happened in my church. Now, I cannot say that I know the reasons for this delay, a delay of some weeks during which the sound of silence was all we heard from the bishops and the Nuncio. Finally, they did send out a message, deploring an attack on a church during a Mass, but mentioning neither the name of the church nor the name of the priest. I believe that this specific silence was a sign of complicity: The Church—the Haitian bishops, the Nuncio, the Vatican—indifferent and cautious, would not mention the name of the priest or the church that had been attacked, because it did not wish to be seen as defending that particular church, that particular priest. The solidarity of the one Church of Jesus Christ Our Lord was destroyed in Haiti by the silence of the bishops and the Nuncio. So easily did they destroy the solidarity that had been built during so many years of resistance to the Duvalier dictatorship.

In any case, it is clear that the massacre in my church was like a lesson written out in blood across the walls of all churches for all to see: It explained in very few words and with very few—but very bloody—pictures what game was being played by the Army and the government, together, their arms wrapped around each other's shoulders and their free hands holding knives, spears, guns, machetes, and the living bowels of children, the children who are the next generation of my people, the children who are the future, the Hope, of my country.

How many times, how many times, brothers and sisters? Have we not already shed enough of our tears? Have they not already spilled enough of our blood? Has the time not already come for us to rise up and refuse their violence? I think that that time has come. I think the time has come for us to say: No more.

The final slap in the face came soon for me, and when it did, I was ready; I had been threatened with it so many times before. My religious order, the Salesians, expelled me from their midst for preaching politics. I can no longer preach in public. As I have said, the crime of which I stand accused is the crime of preaching food for all people. That is what the Salesians and the Haitian bishops and the Vatican (for all of them agreed upon my expulsion) call politics. You should hear them talk, brothers and sisters. They say, clucking and shaking their heads sadly: "Why couldn't he have worked with the poor, distributed food, made a dispensary, opened up a school?" "Tsk, tsk," they say, the sound of an old man condescending to the young. "The role of the pastor," they tell each other, "is to heal the wounds of the suffering. Why could he not do this? Tsk, tsk, tsk."

But I live in Haiti. Haiti is the parish of the poor. In Haiti, it is not enough to heal wounds, for every day another wound opens up. It is not enough to give the poor food one day, to buy them antibiotics one day, to teach them to read a few sentences or to write a few words. Hypocrisy. The next day they will be starving again, feverish again, and they will never be able to buy the books that hold the words that might deliver them. Beans and rice are hypocrisy when the pastor gives them only to a chosen few among his own flock, and thousands and thousands of others starve. Oh yes, perhaps that night, the pastor can sleep better, thinking, "Ti Claude's eyes looked brighter today; I do believe he is growing." Perhaps that will put the pastor's mind at rest. Hypocrisy. Because for every Ti Claude or Ti Bob or Ti Marie to whom the pastor gives his generous bowl of rice and beans, there are a hundred thousand more Ti Claudes, Bobs and Maries, sitting on bony haunches in the dust, chewing on the pit of a mango, finishing their meal for the day. I have seen them, I have seen the children the good pastor never feeds.

What good does it do the peasant when the pastor feeds his children? For a moment, the peasant's anguish is allayed. For one night, he can sleep easier, like the pastor himself. For one night, he is grateful to the pastor, because that night he does not have to hear the whimpers of his children, starving. But the same free foreign rice the pastor feeds to the peasant's children is being sold on the market for less than the farmer's own produce. The very food that the pastor feeds the peasant's children is keeping the peasant in poverty, unable himself to feed his children. And among those who sell the foreign rice are the big landholders who pay the peasant fifty cents a day to work on their fields; among those who profit from the food the pastor gives the peasant's children are the same men who are keeping the peasant in utter poverty, poverty without hope.

Would it not be better—and I ask the question in all humility, in its fullest simplicity—for the peasant to organize with others in his situation and force the large landholders to increase the peasants' pay? Would it not be wiser—more Christian—for the pastor, while he feeds those children, to help the peasant learn to organize? Isn't this a better way to stop the children's cries of hunger forever? As long as the pastor keeps feeding the peasant's children without helping deliver the peasant from poverty, the peasant will never escape the humiliating fate to which he has been assigned by the corrupt system. When the pastor only feeds the children, he is participating in that corrupt system, allowing it to endure. When the pastor feeds the children *and* helps organize the peasants, he is refusing the corrupt system, bringing about its end. Which behavior is more Christian, more evangelical?

I chose the second course, along with many of my colleagues here in the parish of the poor. You have chosen that course, too, brothers and sisters. I chose to help organize youth, I chose to preach deliverance from poverty, I chose to encourage my congregation into hope and belief in their own powers. For me it is quite simple: I chose life over death. I preached life to my congregation, not life as we live it in Haiti, a life of mud, dank cardboard walls, garbage, darkness, hunger, disease, unemployment, and oppression. But life as a decent poor man should live it, in a dry house with a floor and a real roof, at a table with food, free from curable illness, working a meaningful job or tilling the fields to his or her profit, proud.

The only way to preach a decent poor man's life in Haiti is to preach self-defense, defense from the system of violence and corruption that ruins our own and our children's lives. I hope and trust that I have preached self-defense to my people. I would feel myself a hypocrite otherwise. And I would rather die than be a hypocrite, rather die than betray my people, rather die than leave them behind in the parish of the poor.

Open your eyes with me, sisters and brothers. It is morning. The night has been a long one, very long. Now, the dawn seems to be climbing up slowly from beneath the horizon. Wisps of smoke are rising up from the little houses of the village, and you can smell good cornmeal cereal cooking. The sky grows pink. An hour later, the children in their tidy, well-fitting uniforms run off to school, clutching new books in their arms. Women wearing shoes head off to market, some on horseback and donkey, others on motorcycle and bicycle. They all take the new paved road, down which buses take other women and men to market for the day. If you listen closely, you can hear the sound of running water, of faucets being turned on in houses. Then the men emerge, carrying shiny new tools, laughing together, their bodies strong and well fed. They head off for the fields. A new irrigation project has been installed and the crops are growing where before there was almost a desert. Throughout the village, you can hear laughter and the sound of jokes being told and listened to.

This is the village I call Esperancia. The day is coming when this village will exist, though now it is called Despair and its residents wear rags and never laugh. Yet when we look around this village I call Esperancia, we can see that not very much has changed since it was called Despair. This is what has changed: Everyone now eats a decent poor man's breakfast. There is a new road. The children now have books. The women have shoes. There is water, and running water. There is an irrigation project.

This is not very much to change. Yet just those few changes can turn Despair into Hope, and all it takes to change them is organization. In a year, the village of Esperancia could exist in any of our lands. Esperancia, El Salvador; Esperancia, Honduras; Esperancia, Guatemala. It is an honorable address in the parishes of the poor.

Let us leave our old homes of cardboard and mud floors. Let

us make a plan to douse them with gasoline, and burn them to the ground. Let us turn our backs on that great fire and on that way of life, and hand in hand, calmly, intelligently, walk forward into the darkness toward the sunrise of Hope. Let us trust one another, keep faith with one another, and never falter.

Take my hand. If you see me stumble, hold me up. If I feel you weaken, I will support you. You, brother, hold up the lamp of solidarity before us. Sister, you carry the supplies. Yes, the road is long. I fear there are criminals on either side of us, waiting to attack. Do you hear them in the bushes, brothers and sisters? Hush! Yes, I can hear them loading their guns. Let us ignore their threats. Let us be fearless.

Let them come. They do not know it, but though they kill us, though they shoot and cut down every last one of us, there is another battalion about a mile back, coming and coming down this long path toward sunrise. And behind that battalion, another and another and another. God is for the big battalions, and the big battalions are the people. Let us keep the lamp of solidarity lit, and move forward.

Amen.

❖ PART II ❖

SERMONS
AND
MESSAGES

MEV PULEO

A CALL TO HOLINESS

This sermon was delivered at the Cathedral of Port-au-Prince on the Monday before Easter Sunday, 1985. The country was heating up, as opposition to the dictatorship of Jean-Claude Duvalier intensified. There was talk of a general strike during which opposition to the government would coalesce and show its power. —*A.W.*

Jesus is truth. This evening, in the name of that truth, we are going to begin to take a look at a series of issues facing our church. We will do this as we march down the road of holiness to find the Lord, who is holy and who has called us to holiness— a special kind of holiness, during this Holy Week. For this week really to be Holy Week, you and I must try especially hard to become more holy, to take another step toward holiness.

As we find in 1 John 5:6, "It is the Spirit that beareth witness, because the Spirit is truth." We want truth to shine everywhere, we want it to shine while we are trying to grow into holiness, as the Lord God has requested we do. "We are of God: he that knoweth God heareth us; he that is not of God heareth not us. Hereby know we the spirit of truth" (1 John 4:6).

Jesus is truth. In the name of that truth, we speak the truth. Sometimes truth is a bitter pill, and often truth is as bitter as the law, but the truth that we are sharing this evening will not make anyone angry; on the contrary, it will make us more holy, as God has required of us.

Within the church we have many saints, or holy people. Some of the greatest of the saints are canonized: those whom the church recognizes and proclaims after their death. Others die and the church does not proclaim them, nor does it know them officially as saints. If we look up and down in every nook and cranny, we will find that in the church of Jesus Christ there are about 40,000 official saints. Now, when Vatican II—thanks to the Holy Spirit—tried to remake a number of things within the church, there was a rumor that some saints were going to be eliminated from the list. When certain Catholics heard this they felt their faith tremble: the news of truth was hard to bear. The church admitted at that time that there were some among the 40,000 whose history—and even whose existence—it was difficult or impossible to prove.

In any case, the church—thanks to the light of the Holy Spirit ("the Spirit is truth") which illuminates the darkness—removed about forty saints from the ranks. But just because the church removed some of those saints from the list, does this mean that we do not have to walk in the way of saintliness, in the ways of truth? No. The truth is God. God is the source of saintliness.

So we are blessed when we discover that we are not of the darkness but of the light. Beware the person who feels angry upon hearing the words of truth. Hiding the truth is like trying to bury water. It seeps out everywhere.

Out of the 180 saints whom Paul VI proclaimed officially for the universal church, 64 came from Spain, France, and Italy. It makes us feel that the scale is weighted perhaps a little too heavily toward the great nations. If there are, for example, any Haitians officially recognized as saints, we haven't heard about it. And yet there are and have been so many Haitians who are truly holy, and who ought to have been proclaimed as saints for the universal church.

There are saints everywhere. We read that God says to the people of Israel: "Ye shall therefore be holy, because I am holy" (Lev 11:45); and later God tells them: "You shall be holy: for I the Lord your God am holy" (Lev 19:2).

I know you are all happy to hear these words tonight. There are many of us who do not often come up to the altar here at church because we know it is not a very easy thing to take communion. But I think that when you realize that our Father the Lord, our dear Father, calls us to become holy, calls on us truly to live up to his Word, that is when we realize that if we are living out the Word of God really and truly and in truth, then we too may already consider ourselves little saints, worthy to come up to the altar. And as long as you are not proud of your holiness and do not use it to raise yourself up above others, but rather use it to bring others up to holiness, then every day you will become more holy. It's nice to think that tonight the Lord would like to come to us and reproach us, reprimand us for thinking that our sins are so ugly, when he knows that our sins are as nothing.

Long live all of you who feel yourselves crushed beneath the weight of this society! Come to me tonight, because tonight I want to raise you up, I want to help you recognize what you have already become — holy before God. Brothers, sisters, every day we must awake and feel our greatness before men and God. When we say the church is us and we are the church — well, the church has sin within it, so let us purify the church, let us sanctify the church every day. We are people of a church that is already holy; let us make it more holy. Let us put everything that is created in the darkness aside and let holiness grow through prayer.

Beware, however, for there are saints and there are saints. Among us are true saints. But there are false saints also, the unsaintly, the sinful ones; they are full of importance yet insignificant, and they are keeping the poor down, they are stepping on the poor. This is why sometimes it is impossible for us, the poor, to grow toward holiness. The false saints, the insignificant ones, the unholy, are blocking our path. If we do not say this truth, we too risk becoming false saints.

The Bible gives us many examples of these unholy ones: "Have all the workers of iniquity no knowledge, who eat up my people as they eat bread, and call not upon the Lord?"

Now remember, those are not my words. Those of you who have paper and pen, write down the chapter and verse, please: Psalm 14:4. I am not inventing these words, brothers and sisters.

Here are some other things I did not invent: In the factories here, the workers of iniquity pay Haitians seven percent of what they pay people in other countries. Isn't that eating the people? Isn't that sucking the blood of my brothers and sisters who work here, of the poor who work in the factories for the big bosses?

And every time the big capitalist bosses pay out one dollar, they take in four. When they invest $400, they make four times that; when they invest $1,000, they make $4,000. They make a lot of money, while the little that they pay you can barely buy food enough for you and isn't enough to feed your children, to pay for your rent, to pay all your bills. Is it right for these unholy ones—who supposedly invest in our country—to come here and stop us from living? "Shall the throne of iniquity have fellowship with thee, which frameth mischief by a law? They gather themselves together against the soul of the righteous, and condemn the innocent blood" (Psalm 94:20–21).

Here's a little joke:

Once upon a time, there was a big car race taking place. You know, here in Haiti we have a lot of drivers whom you hear about—they like to go fast, fast, fast, without looking where they are going, without checking what's behind them or in front.

Well, this particular race was being held in France, and they asked for a Haitian team to participate, along with representatives from all the countries of the world.

But unfortunately, the people who came to represent Haiti were a band of unholy ones.

When it came time for the race, the Haitian who was driving went fast, fast, fast, but without looking ahead or in back. It turned out he hadn't gone in the right direction . . . so even though he went fast, he still lost the race.

Okay. So everyone said, "Why don't we let the Haitians participate in the reverse race, the backing-up race? And we'll see whether they can win at that."

In the reverse race, they put you in a really terrible position to start with so that it is almost impossible to back up. And that is why the Americans failed. The French got a zero, the Spanish guy, the Chinese guy, they all tried and got nowhere.

So they figured, "Well, if everyone else failed, it sure isn't a Haitian who's going to get a ten."

So one of the team of the unholy Haitians stepped forward.

And they said to him: "Your age?"

And the Haitian said, "I'm 28."[1]

And they said: "Man, you are young. Well, anyway, go on. Go backwards."

And the Haitian didn't even look behind him. With a whoosh, he went backward faster than you could see. And of course he won.

And the judges were amazed.

"You're only 28 years old," they said to him, "and you can make the car go backwards in these terrible conditions?!"

So the Haitian guy says, "Look, for twenty-eight years I've been making a big country like Haiti go backwards, and you think I can't deal with a little car?"

It is this question of backwardness that interests us here in Haiti. "For ye suffer if a man bring you into bondage, if a man devour you, if a man take of you, if a man exalt himself, if a man smite you on the face."

In Leviticus 25:10 we read, "And ye shall hallow the fiftieth year,[2] and proclaim liberty throughout all the land unto all the inhabitants thereof: it shall be a jubilee unto you; and ye shall return every man unto his possession."

That is to say: the Lord recognizes that the earth is for all of God's children. Yet we Haitians, when did we ever own our own land? When? When we were slaves? No. Today? No, even today we hardly own our own land. And amid all this landlessness, we are supposed to grow in saintliness? That is a difficult task, to live with nothing and yet to grow.

Things must change.[3] In Leviticus 25:23, the Lord says: "The land shall not be sold forever: for the land is mine."[4] All the land is the Lord's, and we are all God's children. So the Lord asked all his children, the slaves, not to work the land after a period of seven years. He asked them to call a huge strike, and not to work. And so every seven years, the slaves held a giant strike, a general strike, because they were slaving for the bosses. They were working like donkeys, as the proverb says: The multitude works like a donkey to decorate a few palace horses.

So every seven years the Lord asked his children the slaves to stop their work and hold a strike, and they called that year the *sabatik*, because in Hebrew the number seven is *sheba*. So every seven years, the slaves had a strike, so that they could catch their breath.

Then they decided that every seven years was not enough, and they added every fifty years. And every fifty years they held a strike, and the people who had land had to partition their land with the slaves: they obliged the landlords to redistribute the land. And this year was called the jubilee, the year of grace. Thus we who are slaves must one day share the land—we can feel it in our gut. Because the land is not for a little fistful of gluttons, but for us all.

Thus Isaiah speaks, in chapter 61: "The Spirit of the Lord God is upon me; because the Lord hath anointed me to preach good tidings unto the meek; he hath sent me to bind up the brokenhearted, to proclaim liberty to the captives, and the opening of the prison to them that are bound; to proclaim the acceptable year of the Lord, and the day of vengeance of our God." When Isaiah talks about the acceptable year, that is a reference to the jubilee, the year of grace, the year of liberty and of redistribution of the land. And in Luke 4:18, Jesus reads that same chapter from Isaiah, and Isaiah's words become Jesus' words.

The year of grace. In the year of grace, we do not close our eyes. In the year of grace, we do not fold our arms and wait. The year of grace is not a time for doing nothing. It's not a time in which all you need to do is say "I refuse to obey authority."

The year of grace demands a redistribution of the land. So says the Bible. Someone who does not work to ensure that the children of God have their little land to farm, so that the children of God have a little land to build a house upon, a person who does not work for this, and who does not allow others to work for this, that person is not living in a state of grace, but he is living in a state of sin.

Today we can say that a Christian who wishes to grow in holiness must ask that the land be redistributed. He must ask that the big landholders give land to the poor, and that the poor work that land and make it fruitful. The Lord asks that the state no longer have the poor put their names on papers without knowing what kind of contract they are entering into.

Today, land ownership is an affair like the lottery: you put your name down on a piece of paper, and you have no idea what you're getting into, and no control over the results. For all you know, they tell you you're getting land, when actually the little piece of paper says you're giving it away. And if you're afraid to sign, they beat you. In the book of Proverbs, we find a passage that is very tough, but since it is true, it is the word of God. This is what it says: "As a roaring lion, and a raging bear, so is a wicked ruler over the poor people" (Prov 28:15). Those are not my words. If those words make you feel angry, they're right there in your Bible: rip out the page, but don't try to beat me up, because those are not my words.

To become more holy, to do God's will, Abraham accepted to sacrifice his only son.

And you too, whatever your life may be, whatever your work, whatever your prestige, the only honest and holy route is to be willing to sacrifice all to do the Lord's bidding. And during this sacrifice you may receive many blows. But St. Paul also received many blows because he told the truth and helped people become holy. I expect to receive blows, too, and you must expect that also, even though it is not what we hope for; we must expect it.

St. Paul says: "Thrice was I beaten, once was I stoned, thrice I suffered shipwreck, a night and a day have I been in the deep; in journeyings often, in perils of water, in perils of robbers, in perils by mine own countrymen, in perils by the heathen, in perils in the city, in perils in the wilderness, in perils in the sea, in perils among false brethren; in weariness and painfulness, in watchings often, in hunger and thirst, in fastings often, in cold and nakedness. Beside those things that are without, that which cometh upon me daily, the care of all the churches" (2 Corinthians 11:25–28).

Thus must we expect to suffer to make our church holy, and to do the bidding of the Lord. To do the will of the Lord, you must learn to choose the Lord—or else you choose the devil.

To live a holy life you must make that choice. You cannot be holy and make compromises with Satan. You have to think the way the fellow in Psalm 1 thinks: "Blessed is the man that walketh not in the counsel of the ungodly."

When I was thinking about this psalm, I was praying, and I will tell you how I put the psalm to paper:

"Hallelujah for men and women in Haiti who do not join forces with the malevolent regime. Hallelujah for the Haitians who do not enter into the gluttonous pillaging by a band of the bloodthirsty, in whose midst brother sells brother, in whose midst a brother is not his brother's keeper. Hallelujah, because the path of those Haitians who reject the regime is the path of righteousness and love, and that is what the Lord requires. Where there is beating, breaking, and destruction, the righteous man is not. The way of the Lord is the way of justice, and justice blooms on the banks of Deliverance."

Amen.

WALKING IN THE LIGHT
OF CHRIST

The youth Mass from which these excerpts are taken was said on August 23, 1988, one year after Father Aristide and three other progressive Haitian priests — along with a number of lay people — were ambushed on the national highway at Freycineau. They were stoned, beaten, and threatened with machetes and guns.

All four escaped with relatively minor wounds, but the event proved a turning point in relations within the church. At the time, many progressive clergy and lay people felt that the hierarchy of the church, which had been forced into an uneasy solidarity with Ti Legliz (the progressive or liberation wing of the Church), had failed to speak out on the four priests' behalf at a time of grave need, and had thereby exacerbated the growing battle between the hierarchy and the base of the church.

Several Masses had already been said by Father Aristide in commemoration of the event, and in commemoration of the Ti Legliz hunger strike at the cathedral which preceded the attack.

Two weeks after this Mass was said, a similar youth Mass celebrated by Father Aristide was attacked by a stone-throwing mob thought to be in the pay of the Army and of the mayor of Port-au-Prince. One week later, during a Sunday Mass, Father Aristide's church, St. Jean Bosco, was attacked. At least thirteen congregants were killed, and the church building was burned down. The government in power during the massacre fell the next week.

[Much of this Mass was responsive, but the liberty has been taken of eliding most of the congregation's responses.] —A.W.

Sisters and brothers, good evening.

Since yesterday, we have been walking in the light of Christ

MAGGIE STEBER

within the church of the poor, within the people's church. This morning again we continue to walk in the same light inside the same church. Before we partake of the Mass, we decided that we should celebrate what we have been experiencing over the last two days so that we can continue to experience it within a church ever more robust.

Our celebration will be more beautiful if we sincerely agree to allow the light of Christ to continue to enter into us and to illuminate us, so that we may see our own limitations and our errors and the spaces we have left open for the enemy. When we find those spaces, then we will shut them up, we will avoid our errors and we will build a more solid church, a church more pleasing to Jesus. We will bow our heads before God and ask God please to have pity on us, to listen to our voices, and to pardon us all our sins that may prevent us from seeing our own selves, our own bodies, in the right light, and thus from properly assessing the body of the church, which needs a good cleaning.

We do not really merit the grace of God if we refuse to reflect on the words which we sing here in church. We sing: "Oh Lord, have pity upon us." We sing: "Hallelujah for the Lord in the heavens, we will applaud you, we will celebrate you, we will dance for you."

The Lord has pity upon those who do not understand, but when people begin to understand, when the light of comprehension turns into the light of the Lord—well, he does not give us light for us to make fools of ourselves, for us to sing our song stupidly and without comprehension. We're not going to sing a song that is nonsense.

We say: "In the town of Grand Goave, they're making problems for us, in Hinche, in Papaye. When, oh Father, are we going to live in peace?"

And our Father responds: "You will live in peace when you wrap your faith and your commitment together in a people's church that will permit the people's power to come to a boil in a people's revolution—so that this country can breathe free."

It's the same response he gives when we say to him: In Dichiti they are killing us, in Labadie they are killing us.[5]

"When, oh Lord, are we going to live in peace?" we ask.

And the Lord says to us: "Don't ask me this kind of question any more. Ask yourselves the question: When are we going to wrap our faith and our commitment together to build a people's church with a people's power that will boil over and become a revolution? The ball is at your feet, kick it across the people's field, but don't ask the Lord too many questions."

That is how the Lord speaks with us. He is a Lord of light. And if we accept his light, we will rightly say: Hallelujah to the Lord in the heavens. We will rightly applaud him, we will rightly celebrate him, we will rightly dance for him.

Let us pray.

Oh Lord, our Father, today is August 23, and we all know what that means. The light of liberation within your church has helped us to understand the meaning of that date; it has pushed us to erect the people's camp within the church so that we can make of it a people's church, the church of the poor. And the same light continues to enter into us to illuminate for us the two years that have passed since February 7, 1986.[6] It shows us the machinations that are being concocted inside the church among the hierarchy of the church. When we take stock of everything that is going on, we see that within the church, those of us under the table[7] cannot sit and wait for the hierarchy to offer us some solution to the current impasse.

In order for things to change, for some solution to emerge, we must organize. In order to turn that solution into a reality, we must organize under the table, we must shake the table until it collapses. That way we will be able one day to sit at a new table as brother and sister who have the same Father, who is our Lord; brother and sister who have the same brother, who is Jesus. And that brother is with us today, under the table. He is with us there so that we may escape from under the table, so that one day we can sit at a new table, and eat the food from that table, forever and ever. Amen.

John 9:39–41. This is an important piece of the Bible that we are going to share at this important moment. I ask you all to put yourselves to work to understand what you are going to hear.

John 9:39–41: "For judgment I am come into this world, that

they which see not might see; and that they which see might be made blind."

My friends, let us wag our tongues a little among ourselves and as we talk together, perhaps we will begin to see the meaning of these words. Let us reflect for a moment, each one talking to the one next to him or her. Say what you think, tell your neighbor what you have understood. Without pride, open your hearts to each other, let the Holy Spirit illuminate you. Don't let some inferiority complex make you think you don't understand anything. Put yourself in the hands of the Lord, and he will light you up with the Holy Spirit.

Jesus says he has come into this world for a judgment. This judgment, among whom will it be made? Against whom? Among those who see and those who do not see, those who pretend to see. And if we follow to verse 41, we see which group of people wants to make it seem as though they are the ones who see. The Pharisees.

Now in the time when Jesus lived, at the head of the church there were the Pharisees, and they were the ones who claimed that they bore the light of God within them. Jesus criticized them, saying, You think you see, but soon you shall be as blind.

If Jesus came to Haiti today, on August 23, what would he find? If he looked at the Catholic Church, if he looked at the Protestant Church, if he X-rayed the society, would he say again what he says in John 9:39–41? What reasons are there why Jesus would say of our society what he said of the Pharisees?

If Jesus saw what the hierarchy of the church is doing against Misyon Alfa,[8] he would say the same thing. Those people who believe they see, well, they see so well that they are destroying the Church's literacy program. They say that the program's literacy workers are stupid, unseeing, but it is those literacy workers who were bringing the light, and *they* are the ones who can see.

Are there other instances where Jesus would repeat himself in Haiti today?

Congregation: The massacre at Jean-Rabel.[9]

One participant: It was a bishop who gave the first call for the massacre to begin.

Aristide: Which bishop?

Congregation: Colimon, Colimon, Colimon.[10]

Aristide: Excuse me. I thought the church was a place where there were people who pray all day and all night, like Bishop Colimon. How could a man like that do such a thing?

Congregation: (much conversation).

Aristide: Okay, well, I'll respect what you say. Let's continue. Are there any other cases where you think Jesus would repeat what he says in John 9:39–41?

Congregation: The attack at Freycineau.

Aristide: But at Freycineau, it was the Papal Nuncio who came to get us to take us home safely.

Congregation: (shouting in protest).

Aristide: Ah! Okay, excuse me, I thought that the bishops also said that they were against what happened at Freycineau. But the way you're talking there, I'm starting to ask myself a couple of questions. Help me find the answer. The way you're talking, it's like, I don't know, it's as though you meant to say: If at Freycineau all four of the priests and all the lay people had died, the bishops would have been happy? Is that what you mean?

Congregation: Yes, yes, yes!

Aristide: Wait, wait. The Lord does not like calumny. The Lord does not want us to tell tales. Let's see whether what you're saying has any foundation, or if it is just general emotion or feeling. What makes you say that they would have been happy last year, if we had died in the attack. Had we wronged them?

Congregation: (much conversation).

Aristide: The group of people you're talking about, the bishops, are there no exceptions among them? Who are the exceptions?

Congregation: Bishop Romélus, Bishop Poulard . . .

Aristide: Who else?

Congregation: Bishop Lafontant.[11]

Aristide: Any more?

Congregation: No.

Aristide: Fine, okay. Okay, so we're going to do as Jesus did: We are going to distinguish among the Pharisees, and we are going to let the light of the Holy Spirit shine on us as it shone on Jesus, so that we do not make any false judgments. ... We don't pretend that we are like Jesus, that we have no faults, that we have no sin. We just don't want evil tongues to speak against us. We agree that Jesus is the Lord, and that because he is Lord, he can come unto us in order to make us speak correctly. We will be precise so that evil tongues will not speak against us, will not say that we are taking it upon ourselves to judge the bishops. We are not judging the bishops, we are simply making a judgment. I am come into the world for a judgment, Jesus said, and we too want to make a judgment, but we do not want to judge the bishops.

For example, we have seen that we can't put all the bishops in the same basket. Now, can we put all the priests in it? All the nuns?

Congregation: No.

Aristide: Don't you think that they will say that we are trying to divide the church, that we are trying to divide the priests and the nuns?

Congregation: Yes.

Aristide: Is it because we have a devil in our hearts that we are trying to divide priest from priest, or is it because we do not want to accept lies that we are making this sort of distinction?

We don't want to accept lies, we want to live in truth. So let us resume: There are bishops, priests, and nuns who dine at the table, and then there are bishops, priests, and nuns who huddle under the table.

Those who are at the table, from which social class do they come? We find the majority of them in the class called the bourgeoisie,[12] and in the Army. Now the majority of soldiers are born under the table, but the system turns them into sycophants and flatterers and kept-boys who sit at the table next to their masters.

Today, we want to be Jesus' disciples. Jesus says: I am come into the world for a judgment, and then there he stands facing the Pharisees, and he says: This class of people sit at the table — if he were here, that is the word he might use, they sit at the table — and they believe that they can see. Because they believe they are the ones with true sight, they think they can give us orders when they want. They think they can send us to vote in elections when they want. They think they can send us to vote for a constitution when they want. They think they can tell us not to make a revolution.

They think they can send us to conduct a dialogue with a general who is driving the train of state into a tunnel where there are bodies and blood. And then, when we say no, they say, it's because we are stupid, because we don't understand, because we are illiterate, because we cannot see.

Now, we don't say that we are the only ones who can see the truth. Simply put: We are marching behind Jesus who is the truth. And whenever they tell us lies, we will say to them: Lies!

Today, one year to the day after the attack at Freycineau, we tell the truth. We will fight to defend that truth. God who witnesses this will always stay under the table with the people. He declares that from now on, the church that walks in truth cannot remain under the control of the church that sits at the table. The church that walks in truth cannot sit with its head bowed before that other church. The church below—this is not another separate church, a power parallel to that of the bishops. No. Rather, it is *our* church, Jesus' church, God's church. And God asks that a conversion take place among those who sit at the table of privilege, so that God's light may shine on them also, so that one day, *all* of us may find ourselves upending the table.

Let the truth of the Lord be a purgative that cleans out all the old ways of the bourgeoisie, all the old ways of the Army that flatters and does the bidding of the Americans. We are tired of hearing the bourgeois leaders whispering in our ears with their little voices saying, "Come on with us, come on," trying to make us their accomplices. This old corrupt class is bathed in corruption. It has endured for two centuries and should not last any longer. Enough.

The bishops will say: Ah, you are too hard on us. They will say we are arrogant. We will tell them that it is God who demands that the church be controlled in part by the majority. The poor have sacrificed for this church, the church of Haiti, and so it is normal for them to speak loudly about it, it's normal for them to cry out. For history has taught that beautiful words do not make a revolution. Inside the church, sweet and pretty words do not always bring about the changes that the Lord wishes.

The Haitian church is lucky because of its youth, who stand there with truth in their hands; these young people will no longer agree to live a lie. The Haitian church is lucky because these young people say that they will no longer participate in the bourgeois church. No, they want to live in the church of the poor. Puebla [the 1979 meeting of the Latin American bishops] says: The Lord has chosen us to make an option for the poor.

The Lord has chosen us to tie our fates to the fate of the poor. It is you, the youth, who enable the church of Haiti to bear that name: the church of the poor, the popular church, the people's church. Vatican II says: The church is the people of God.

We must not fear the word "popular."[13] The church is the popular church, the people's church. We must not reconcile ourselves to all the corrupt ways of the society.

After all, did the Lord send Moses to praise Pharaoh?

The Lord recognized that Moses was powerful because of Moses' connection to the people and their power. The Lord knows that the power of God's servant is connected to the power of the people. Those who carry the demands of the people in their hands are one with the people. His enemies could not devour Jesus, because he was one with the people; they were behind him. When the people are there, God is there. God speaks through the people's voice.

The Lord said to Moses: You are the voice of the people. Fight Pharaoh, break the chain of slavery.

The Lord says to me today: The Haitian people, the church of the poor, the popular church, they are all risen. Continue the battle.

Even if they kill two, three, four—continue to fight. They may massacre many. . . . Stand up, and keep fighting.

We are a people who stand up, and we keep fighting, with another Moses leading us, with many Moseses, who go forward to break the chains, to denounce the Pharisees, to trace the design of deliverance[14] which will call up a revolution that will change Haiti for once and for all. Amen.

The church of the poor is under the protection of the flag of liberation theology, which cannot be disconnected in Haiti from the nationalist courage that manifests itself in actions, good actions, and in the organization that brings those actions to pass. So let us sing the national anthem.

Let's not sing just to sing, let's not sing to show we know our little bit of culture, let's not sing to show off.

Let's sing with the conviction which we must have, and which we have begun to demonstrate.

We are poor, it is true, but we have pride. We are poor, it is true, but we are courageous. We are poor, it is true, but we are people nonetheless. We know that the Lord created us in his image, and we the poor, who are abused, who are mistrusted, we are proud to be made in God's image. That pride will make us fight like the armies of God until the light of deliverance appears.

So let us make that light of deliverance appear. If you are a Haitian, if you have Haitian blood that runs in your veins, if you are a real Haitian, stand beneath the flag of conviction, and sing the national anthem. Link your faith with your commitment, not like unwitting children, but like the proud Christians that you are.

(The congregation sings the national anthem.)

Let us pray for the pope. There are people who say that we have split from Pope John Paul II. We say: No. But Pope John Paul II must respect the word of truth that we are sharing in Haiti just as we ourselves must respect him and his words. We share the words of truth, and perhaps those words will shed a little light on his world, just as, if he shares those words truly, then that sharing will shed a little light on our world. We are the sisters and the brothers of the pope. We have the same father, who is our Lord.

We pray also for all the bishops of the Haitian church. We love them, and we cannot lie to them, and we ask them not to lie to us.

We pray also for Father Jean-Marie Vincent, Father William

Smarth, Father Antoine Adrien.[15] Only the Lord knows why he gave us such a miracle of escape.

We pray also for all nuns, especially Sister Roselène, who was with us that day. And we don't forget the rest of the people who were with us, even if we do not cite their names.

And we ask the Lord to bless Bishop Romélus, Bishop Poulard, Bishop Lafontant.

Jesus, if we work to love our enemies, then how could we come to hate the bishops? We love them. But we love to tell the truth. We do not love everything the bishops do. We cannot applaud them unless we like what they do. We cannot lie while we are at prayer.

We are praying to you that the people's church, in spite of all it has to bear, may find a way to avoid discouragement. We pray that when the people's church grows discouraged—if it does grow discouraged—that we may find a way to regain our spirits, without losing our way. Let us bow our heads.

I have come into the world for a judgment, to make a distinction, to create a division. That is what Jesus said. It was in order to create a real unity that Jesus divided those who accept the truth from those who refuse it. The Pharisees refused the truth; Jesus put them aside. It is the same evangelical power that causes us to speak the way we speak and act the way we act. The will of Jesus was to gather all of his little ones together—in unity and in truth. And the will of the people's church is to create the same unity—not a unity in untruth, but a unity in truth. Then we will be able to worship Jesus who helps us build unity in truth, who helps us construct the church of those who love truth.

Amen.

"WE HAVE COME FROM FAR AWAY"

This message was broadcast on Radio Soleil three weeks after Father Aristide's church was burned to the ground and his congregants massacred (September 11, 1988) by men thought to be in the pay of Port-au-Prince mayor Franck Romain and a section of the Haitian Army, led by the then-president, Gen. Henri Namphy. A week after that attack, Gen. Prosper Avril overthrew Gen. Namphy in a coup d'etat (September 17) ostensibly organized by progressive noncommissioned officers disgusted with the church massacre and Gen. Namphy's reported complicity in the attack.

The day before this message was broadcast, Father Aristide had been informed—incorrectly, as it turned out—that in spite of a wave of rumors to the contrary, his church was to be rebuilt, and he was to be allowed to remain at St. Jean Bosco, within his religious congregation.

[The word netwayaj *in Creole—which means "clean-up"— was given to the popular movement against corruption that followed Avril's coup d'etat.]*   —A.W.

> Sisters and brothers,
> Valiant youth of Haiti,
> Parents and friends of the victims of the massacre
>   at St. Jean Bosco,
> I salute you, and I thank you with all my heart.
> I bow low before your courage and I greet you
> With honor and respect.
> Honor and respect for all of you:
> Friends here and friends abroad,

MEV PULEO

Brave Christians, progressive Vodouisants,
Comrades who believe in God, and those who do
   not—
Honor, and respect!

Honor and respect for the compassionate spirit that
   has allowed me to keep my mandate to work with
   the Lord in the midst of the people.
The messages that usually come from Rome ask for
   my departure.
The most recent one, however, has accorded me the
   right to remain here among you.
For how long?
A mystery.

I am ready to obey both the Lord, the Salesian provincial
delegate, and the people of God, with all my heart. This willingness is based on the spirit of love that has always existed
between me and the Salesian provincial—we have always been
as one in the hand of God, as one in the midst of Haitian youth,
as one in the church of the poor here in Haiti.

What a marvel when we love one another!
Because Jesus loved the poor, he sacrificed his life
   for them.
Because the victims of the massacre at St. Jean Bosco
   were bathed in love,
      they fell like Jesus for the deliverance of our
      nation.

Yes, the Bible is right to say "Thou shalt love thy
   neighbor as thyself" (Lev 19:18).
And there is no greater proof of love than accepting
   to die for someone you love (cf. John 3:16).

In my prayers, I continue to kneel before the courage
of all those victims.
They live in my heart, in my blood, in my memory.

On Sunday, the eleventh of September, our prayers
rose up.
Seven days later, grace descended.
On the Sunday of the eighteenth, grace appeared like
the morning light of an Easter Sunday.
The Work of God. God is light (John 1:5).

His light was rising up, and the clean-up began.
The sun began to shine, it shone upon the valiant
soldiers who put their shoulders to the clean-up
operation, the valiant soldiers whom I salute with
respect today.

At Mass on Good Friday of last year, I washed the feet of a
soldier to remind us that the role of a military man is to bow
down before the people, to wash the feet of the people, and not
to wash his own feet in the blood of that people.

But today, I am more disposed to kiss the feet of all the
valiant and patriotic soldiers who have chosen to remain in the
people's camp, who have chosen to continue the clean-up operation until we overthrow the table of privilege and corruption
where the elite are feasting.

The light is spreading to help me understand the depth of
the words Jesus speaks in John 15:6. He says: He who is not
one with me, they will cut him down and throw him away; he
will dry up like a branch of wood. And when the branches are
dry, they gather them, they cast them into the fire, they burn
them.

I repeat: John 15:6.
I repeat again: John 15:6.

This is called an evangelical clean-up, a prophetic clean-up. This clean-up must proceed *where* it needs to proceed and *when* it needs to proceed, and *in the ways* in which it needs to proceed.

> Where should the clean-up go forward?
> Everywhere. In all four corners of the country.
> How should it proceed?
> Gently, or with the arms of the people's soldiers—
> without abuse, without injustice.
> When should it be done?
> Soon, soon—without hotheadedness.
> Fast, fast—without disorder.

My people:

—Do you believe that before the seventeeth of October, one month to the day after the seventeenth of September and Dessalines Day[16], Fort Dimanche[17] cannot be clean?

—Do you believe that before the seventeenth of October, Franck Romain cannot be brought before the people of La Saline[18] to be judged in accordance with the law in a people's court?

—Do you believe that before the seventeenth of October, they don't have time to detach the *attachés*[19] who are hidden with their heavy arms; to disarm, arrest, and begin to judge in an extraordinary trial all the criminals who are soaked through with the massacres at Fort Dimanche, Jean-Rabel, Danty, Ruelle Vaillant, Labadie, St. Jean Bosco, and the assassinations of Louis-Eugene Athis, Yves Volel, Lafontant Joseph,[20] and the rest?

—Do you believe that before the seventeenth of October, they cannot clean up the government-run television and radio stations?

—Do you believe that before the seventeenth of October, schoolchildren and university students cannot be given a little of the justice they deserve, after having suffered so many blows?

— Do you believe that before the seventeenth of October, the toxic waste dump in Gonaïves, the toxic Macoutes who are running the rural sections, and all the poisonous sheriffs, magistrates, and judges, and all the toxic waste dumps of the state bureaucracy cannot begin to disappear in order that they may never ever reappear again?

General-President, it's your turn.
Many valiant soldiers have taken their turn.
Many Duvalierist ministers have lost the game.
It's your turn to play, before a people
who have no confidence in you.

It's your turn before a people
who must consider
all of the great Duvalierists as great criminals
until they prove otherwise — for the rest of their lives.

Sergeant Hebreux[21], and all my Haitian brothers who form the base of the Haitian Army, allow me to remind you:

1. The seventeenth of October is not far off.

2. The Duvalierist officers who have been discharged are waiting for the rank-and-file of the Army at the crossroads, with their swords drawn, ready to fight to the death.

3. The U.S. government, along with its lackeys among the Haitian elite, has already begun to conspire to infiltrate Macoutes into the Army, to buy off soldiers, to sow corruption, to plant divisions, and to multiply spies.

4. The Army's rank-and-file and the Haitian people must tie themselves together in a great and solid chain, so that no boss or leader can rope us into dictatorship.

A solid organization among the Palace guards, the guards of the Dessalines Barracks, the guards of the General Headquarters, and the guards of the Leopard Unit must grow like the horns of an angry bull.

When the bull knows his own force, he will let no one yoke him into servitude.

5. If the Duvalierist officers and the two or three Macoutes who have been forcibly removed and all the others who ought to be removed—if they are not brought before the people's court, we may well say that we have been April Fools.[22] The election drums are sounding, and for what kind of elections? Without judgment, many of the criminals will return to the polling place, even more demonic, to drink the people's blood, to kill people, to burn, to empty guns into radio stations, to fire on rectories, to hunt down priests, to hunt down lay people, to persecute the organizations of the people.

Brothers and sisters, I pray to God that we keep our eyes steady in the light of the Holy Spirit, and that we not mistake what is now glittering for gold.

I am here to cry out to you and to remind you that:

> We have come from far away in order to arrive at a
> remote destination.
> We have left the ravine of death in order to arrive
> at the top of the mountain of life.

> Are we there yet?
> No.
> Do we want to get there?
> Yes.
> Can we get there?
> Yes.

We have come from far away in order to arrive at a
remote destination.
When we get there, we will plant the will of the
people.
The will of the people is the will of God.
We have come from far away in order to arrive at a
remote destination.

When we get to our destination, we will organize
ourselves
so that we may cease threading eyeless needles in the
dark.
Yes, we have come from far away in order to arrive
at a remote destination.

When we get to that distant point
We will have made a worthy revolution.
We will have upset the table of privilege so that we
too will be welcome to sit and eat.
We have come from far away in order to arrive at a
remote destination.
We want to get there.
We can get there.
We will get there,
in the name of Jesus who has helped us
come all that great distance to arrive at our rightful
destination,
Amen.

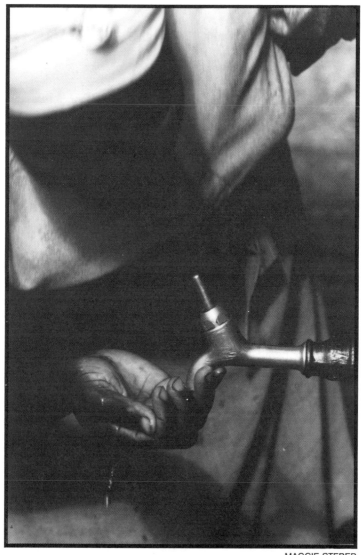

MAGGIE STEBER

LET THE FLOOD DESCEND

This message was delivered on Radio Haiti-Inter in November 1988, two months after Gen. Avril came to power in the coup d'etat that deposed Gen. Namphy. Avril's takeover was presented to the Haitian people as having been initiated by a group of progressive noncommissioned officers disgusted with the burning and sacking of Father Aristide's church a week before the coup occurred. However, the promise of the September coup d'etat was never realized. Though many of the young sergeants wanted Gen. Avril to install a constitutional government, he instead hardened his rule and eventually imprisoned and then discharged the men who had been responsible for bringing him to power.

A general strike against Avril — called by the nation's largest labor union — had been observed on the day that this message was delivered, although Avril announced beforehand that he considered such a strike unconstitutional and illegal.

Meanwhile, the thread attaching Father Aristide to his religious order, the Salesians, was stretching ever thinner. With approval from the Haitian bishops, the order was getting ready to oust him. First they ordered him to leave Haiti. One week after this message was broadcast, 10,000 people took to the streets to prevent Father Aristide from departing. All access to the airport was cut by the demonstrators. Aristide remained in Haiti. Three weeks later, he was officially expelled from the Salesian order.   *—A.W.*

To my sisters, my brothers,
To all my brothers and sisters in the Good Lord
Who raise their voices together with us,
To the valiant youth of Haiti,

101

To the peasants—whether Catholic, Protestant, or
Vodouisant—
To the brave Haitians abroad,
To the courageous Haitians here in Haiti,
And to all of you who have just achieved a legal
general strike
In spite of the declarations of an illegal General:
Hats off to you,
Congratulations on your courage.

Courageously, you stand up, and you speak.
Courageously, you stand up, and you do not give way.
I see all this.
I see you speaking for the Lord.
I hear the Lord's voice in your voice.
I am watching you rise up here and abroad
So that I may be permitted to stay with you here in
Haiti
—and to be with you who are abroad.

A beautiful inspiration from the Holy Spirit!
A beautiful declaration of brotherly love, a declara-
tion
Which invites me to look you in the eye, my sisters
and brothers,
And to say to you what Jesus would have said to you
In his language: *Ani ohev otha, ani ohev ota'kh.*
I love you.

You who have plotted against me,
You who have plotted against the Haitian people:
Bishop Paolo Romeo, Bishop Gayot, Bishop
Ligondé,

Bishop Kebreau and the rest,
Let me look you in the eye,
Please, don't be ashamed.
Look me in the eye.
I have come to tell you: I love you, too.
Because I love you, I must tell you the truth.
Truth and love are the same.
Truth and love are Jesus in the midst of the poor.

What luck for the Haitian church,
Rich, thanks to the poor,
In a country that is poor because of the rich.
The church is rich thanks to us, the poor
Who ceaselessly demand the truth
From every corner.

What luck for the Haitian church,
Rich, thanks to the poor,
In a country that is poor because of the rich.

The church is rich thanks to us, the poor,
Who have stopped certain bishops
(Hidden behind the sins they commit)
When they try to tell lies,
To conspire together
And to create silence.

What luck for the Haitian church,
Rich, thanks to the poor,
In a country that is poor because of the rich.

The church is rich thanks to us, the poor,
Who have agreed to be a part of one sole body

In order to avoid the monolith of a head without a
body.

Alone, we are weak.
Together, we are strong.
Together, we are the flood.

Let the flood descend, the flood of
Poor peasants and poor soldiers,
The flood of the poor jobless multitudes (and poor
soldiers),
Of poor workers (and poor soldiers),
The flood of all our poor friends (and all the poor
soldiers) and
The church of the poor, which we call the children
of God!
Let that flood descend!
And then God will descend and put down the mighty
and send them away,
And He will raise up the lowly and place them on
high (cf. Luke 1:52).

To prevent the flood of the children of God from
descending,
The imperialists in soutane have conspired with the
imperialists of America.
This is why we Haitians must say to one another what
Jesus declared (Mark 2:11):
Arise! Go forth! Walk!

Yes, arise and go forth. Walk.
Arise and go forth so that the Tontons Macoute will
stop walking in ways wet with our blood.
Arise and go forth so that the criminals will stop
walking upon us.

Arise and go forth so that the assasins will stop wak-
ing us in our beds with rounds of gunfire.

Too much blood has been spilled!
Too many of the innocent have fallen!
This is too much for us.

General Avril, you have said: Haiti is debased.
And then? And then, nothing!
You said you would close the infamous prison, Fort
Dimanche.
And then? And then, nothing!
The people are hungry. Misery inhabits their bones.
Your arms are turned against them.
Wait! you say to the people.

The workers are in trouble. The schools are falling
apart. The universities are in shreds.
Wait! you say.

The peasantry is trapped with nowhere to go. But
the rural sheriffs are doing just fine.
Just hold on! you tell the people. Why are you all in
such a hurry? you ask them.

St. Jean Bosco burned to the ground. Franck Romain
on the prowl.
Mr. Avril supporting him.
Wait! says Avril to the people.

The little boss is on the payroll of the big boss. The
big boss is on the Americans' payroll.
Ah, ah, ah. . . . Wait! you tell us.

I'm trying to fix this car, General Avril says.
I'm trying to fix it, and then you all come along and

stick your hands in the engine. You're going to get
hurt, he tells us.
Just sit back and wait! Avril says.

Slavery in the Army.
Slavery in the Dominican Republic.[23]
Too bad! you say to the people. Just wait a little.

One coup d'etat. Another coup d'etat.
One general goes. Another takes his place.
And then? And then, nothing!

Wait?
Until when?
Until the cows come home and pigs fly.

General Avril,
The people's court is right:
Your government is guilty and powerless.
You are guilty
   because you have allowed the savage Tontons
   Macoute to run wild
with no cord of justice around their necks.
You are guilty
   because you have refused to tie the cord of justice
   around the necks of Franck Romain and the other
   men who massacre.
You are guilty
   because you betray the soldiers who brought you
   to power,
   because you discharge patriotic soldiers,
   because you protect corrupt soldiers.

You are guilty
   because before justice is done, you want to send

the people to die in sham elections, just to satisfy
the American government.

You are guilty
because you are playing François Duvalier's game.

You are powerless
because your government gets:
Zero points for justice;
Zero points for public security,
And only one point for clean-up—you got rid of
Namphy.

General Avril, can't you see that the train that
derailed Namphy is going to go off the tracks even
faster with you if, before November 29,[24] you do
not:
Free the patriotic soldiers, arrest the Macoutes,
Lock up Franck Romain, clean out corruption,
And end insecurity in the streets?

The matter is in your hands.
The people will write their own fate.
The blessing of God is upon them. Thus, grace will
descend until the flood brings down
All Duvalierists
All Macoutes
All criminals
Forever and ever.
Amen.

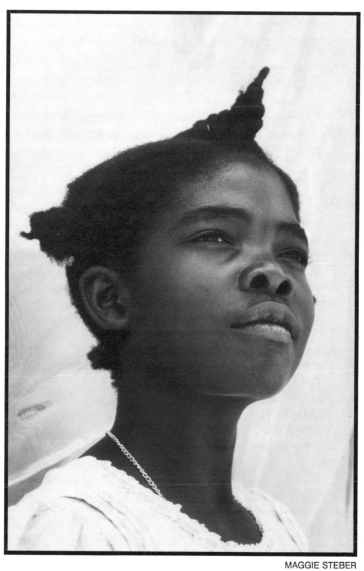

MAGGIE STEBER

NOTES

1. Jean-Claude Duvalier was 28 in 1985.

2. Father Aristide may have been referring to the recent fiftieth anniversary of the end of the U.S. occupation of Haiti.

3. When he visited Haiti in 1983, Pope John Paul II, in speaking of the disparity between the wealthy and the poor in Haiti, said, "Things must change."

4. From Haitian independence in 1804 up to the beginning of the U.S. occupation of Haiti in 1915, every Haitian constitution had declared that no foreigner could own land in Haiti. During the occupation, Franklin D. Roosevelt, then undersecretary of the U.S. Navy, rewrote the Haitian constitution to allow foreign proprietership. Because the initial stage of Haitian history was concerned primarily with ownership of land (slaves taking the land from the masters), land ownership has always been a volatile issue in Haiti, and land reform has been the top priority of the progressive clergy and of the progressive opposition for the past fifteen years.

Aristide is intertwining two themes in this section: the importance of taking back the land—which is still largely and often illegally held by absentee landlords and friends of former presidents—and the general strike.

5. In Grand Goave (see previous paragraphs), various popular groups were attacked by conservative forces that summer; in Hinche and Papaye, organizers of the Peasant Movement of Papaye were harassed by the authorities; members of youth movements from Dichiti and Labadie were also harassed by army and police authorities in the Artibonite region, and four had been killed that summer.

6. Jean-Claude Duvalier was overthrown and fled Haiti on this date.

7. A favorite metaphor of Father Aristide's. In 1986, he composed a poem about the fall of Duvalier and its aftermath called "Leve Tabla," or "Up-end the Table." In the universe of this poem, all the poor

and exploited are beneath a large table filled with food, from which the elite and the privileged are eating. The image of a table overflowing with food has power in Haiti, the poorest country in the hemisphere. The overturning of this table of privilege by the people who huddle beneath it is Father Aristide's metaphor for the overthrow of the current system in Haiti.

8. In the summer of 1988, the bishops decided to close Misyon Alfa, the church literacy campaign, for "restructuring." In the two years it operated after Jean-Claude Duvalier's fall, Misyon Alfa had grown enormously. It was receiving hundreds of thousands of dollars from North American and European donors. The program was extremely popular, both with city slumdwellers and with peasants, and it was introduced through the ecclesial base communities, or Ti Legliz. But since 1987, the program had come under constant attack from the regime. The most famous disappearance in the post-Duvalier years was that of a Misyon Alfa worker, Charlot Jacquelin.

When the bishops dismantled the program, therefore, it was seen as a blow against Ti Legliz specifically, and against Haiti's popular movements in general. The restructured program has not gained the confidence of foreign donors, and the program was virtually nonexistent as of 1990.

9. In July 1987, in the northern provincial city of Jean-Rabel and its environs, more than 200 peasants involved in land-reform actions were massacred by forces allied to the government and large local landholders.

10. Bishop Colimon is the bishop of the Northwest Province where Jean-Rabel is located.

11. These three were bishops who at the time were perceived as more progressive than their colleagues in the nine-man Episcopal Conference of Haiti.

12. *Bourgeoisie,* in Haiti, has come to mean the class that Western Europeans would consider the *haute bourgeoisie,* or the elite.

13. There had been a confrontation the year before between Ti Legliz and the hierarchy over the use of the term "l'église populaire" by progressive priests and other religious.

14. In Creole, *vèvè delivrans. Vèvè* are the drawings made by the priests of *vodun* (or voodoo) to attract and announce the gods at a ceremony.

15. These were the three other priests who were riding with Father Aristide a year earlier, when his car was ambushed at Freycineau.

16. Jean-Jacques Dessalines was a leader of the revolution that

gained independence for Haiti in 1804. He is considered one of the nation's founding fathers.

17. Fort Dimanche is the prison made notorious by the Duvaliers. In their day, it was known primarily as a penitentiary for political prisoners, and was infamous for its complete negligence of the majority of prisoners — many of whom starved to death within its walls — and for its summary executions, its torture chambers, its mass burial grounds. After the fall of Jean-Claude Duvalier in 1986, a movement was started to close Fort Dimanche as a prison and turn it into a memorial to the murdered political prisoners. Four years later, it was finally closed.

18. La Saline is one of Port-au-Prince's largest slums. It runs along the seaside avenue, and extends to Grande Rue, the capital's main street. Father Aristide's church, St. Jean Bosco, was at the outer edges of La Saline.

19. *Attachés* were civilians, often former members of the Tontons Macoute, who were recruited and armed by various units of the Army for paramilitary work, often on death squads.

20. On April 26, 1986, there was a massacre of demonstrators in front of Fort Dimanche (see pp. 40ff). No one was ever arrested in connection with the attack. On July 23, 1987, more than two hundred peasants demonstrating for land reform were massacred in the northwest town of Jean-Rabel. No one was ever arrested in connection with the attack. At Danty and Labadie, peasants and youth group members were killed by members of the rural constabulary. No one was ever arrested in connection with the attacks. On November 29, 1987, more than 17 voters were killed in an all-out attack on a polling place at Ruelle Vaillant in Port-au-Prince. Within the hour, the elections — Haiti's first in three decades — were cancelled. No one was ever arrested in connection with the attack. Before that bloody election day, two prominent and likely presidential candidates, Athis and Volel, were assassinated by elements associated with Gen. Namphy's military government. No one was ever arrested in connection with those murders. In July 1988, Lafontant Joseph, a lawyer and human-rights activist, was assassinated and his body dumped near the airport road. No one was ever arrested in connection with the attack.

21. Sgt. Joseph Hebreux, who was considered at the time of Gen. Avril's coup to be one of the principal progressive noncommissioned officers leading the takeover, later proved to be Avril's lackey who finally grew insubordinate at the end of the general's rule and was assigned out of the presidential palace.

22. In Creole, *pwason davril*. Literally translated, this means "the

fish of April." Because the word for the month of April in French and Creole is Avril, the same as Gen. Prosper Avril's last name, the phrase *pwason davril*—with its connotation of fools and being fooled or taken in—was used as a common street pun to imply that the people had been duped by President Avril.

23. A reference to the thousands of Haitians who cut cane in the neighboring Dominican Republic each year.

24. The anniversary of the 1987 election-day massacre.